Spiritual

Harvest

Spiritual Harvest

William Allen LePar

Discourses on the Path to Fulfillment
Edited by Don Weisgarber

Published by SOLAR Press
P.O. Box 2276
North Canton, OH 44720

Cover illustration copyright © 1998 by Don Weisgarber
Designed by Don Weisgarber

Library of Congress Catalog Card Number: 97-61832
ISBN 1-885728-01-8
Printed in the United States of America

contents

Allons! we must not stop here,
However sweet these laid-up stores, however
    convenient this dwelling we cannot remain here,
However shelter'd this port and however calm these
    waters we must not anchor here,
However welcome the hospitality that surrounds us
    we are permitted to receive it but a little while.

WALT WHITMAN

Foreword

To benefit fully from this book the reader must be open to the idea that there are influences from beyond our physical world. That such influences can be for good or bad is a dilemma, and we must rely on our God-given wisdom to tell the difference. If they drive a wedge between us and our God and push us farther from Him, we can be pretty sure they are of a negative nature. But if they draw us closer, and cause us to become better people (we know inherently when we are growing better and when we are growing worse) then we can rely on a belief that the source of that guidance is good. The proof is in the results, in the way that our lives have changed for the better.

For most of us here on earth the influences from the spiritual realms are subtle. If we recognize them at all, they take the form of vague sensations or feelings: we feel better after we pray and have been helped in some way; we feel a pang of conscience for having done something we know to be wrong; we unaccountably avoided an accident that surely would have killed us but for the grace of something unknown; we turned to just the right passage in the Bible in a time of sorrow. We are not geared to receiving guidance from the spiritual realms directly. It must be slipped past our guards, so to speak—behind our backs, when we aren't looking. Because to accept such influences directly goes against our scientifically trained minds. The "real" world, we can't help believing, consists of physical laws and self-reliance. We shut out the spiritual world just beyond our senses and thereby miss out on its direct assistance. Yet in spite of the many who are unreceptive, there are some people who have not closed themselves to spiritual influence. They have left the door open to guidance from a spiritual realm beyond the physical world, and not just guidance for themselves, but for others as well. Such is the case with William LePar, the author of the essays in *Spiritual Harvest*.

As I said, the full benefit of these essays depends on belief in at least the possibility of an influence from beyond our world. But this is not absolutely necessary—you may believe they were dreamed up in the mind of one man. It is still very worthwhile reading. The luster fades a little though if the spiritual influence is discounted. After all, the Ten Commandments would hardly have had the impact that they did if Moses had penned them himself. But even if he had, their principles would still hold true. And so do the ideas presented in this book. You may find yourself wondering, "And just how in the world could the author know that?" in reference to some seemingly preposterous idea or fact. And that is where you may have to induce Coleridge's "willing suspension of disbelief." If you do not believe in a spiritual influence in these chapters, you may have to temporarily suspend your disbelief about what the author can know.

A consistency of theme runs throughout this book. The road to spiritual growth is not a soft one nor a winding one. Though there may be more than one path to the ultimate goal, the paths do not meander at the traveler's pleasure. Spiritual growth is tough and demanding, and often it does not feel good. It takes self-discipline and sometimes self-denial, concepts that are not too popular in our society. The author has little sympathy for the seeker who wants to be told what a great job he is doing. More often the reader will find out about himself what he needs to know—where he is failing. And yet the very fact that one is reading a book on spirituality, has invested personal time taken out of a busy life, is an indication that the right road has been chosen. One does not read spiritual books to avoid spirituality, as one might read a book on bankruptcy to avoid financial failure. It is not an accident that you have chosen this book—it is an indication that at a higher level of your being you quite possibly are anticipating the next level of growth, and are willing to risk looking at yourself more closely, with a clearer sight. But where along the spiritual path is the reader? This book provides guideposts.

It would be only fair to explain, to the extent possible, in what manner the author has been influenced by the spiritual world. You don't have to search very far into literature to see that he is in good company. Contact with the spiritual world is not an unusual occurrence, even among literary giants: William Wordsworth, who spent much of his literary career lamenting a loss of contact with the spiritual world as he grew older; William Blake, the English author, painter, and mystic; Walt Whitman, who not only wrote about the spiritual world, but wrote of himself as being the spiritual embodiment of America; and there are other figures such as Thoreau, C.S. Lewis, and De La Mare. At one time I thought these mystical writers were drawing from their imaginations for the impression it would leave on their readers. That was before I realized just how very close the spiritual world is to some people. It is right *there* to them, and their only difficulty is how to communicate that existence to others—not just to tell them about it, but to let them feel its presence.

The main difference, as I see it, between the many authors who have written about the mystical or spiritual experience and LePar is this: He writes at the time of, and because of, the contact with the world beyond the physical. For him it is not a euphoric feeling of Oneness that he attempts to recapture, but it is a direct contact, a direct link to the spiritual realm from which he receives his insight. Once he is in the proper state of mind the ideas and words flow to him and through him. It is as if a radio comes on within him and the information he receives is passed on to be written down. Who knows how such an event can happen? We in the material world have enough trouble explaining physical laws of nature, and are out of our league in trying to decipher the workings of the spiritual world. And who is to say for certain if the information so obtained is from LePar's higher self or from an even higher spiritual source? The soul of each individual exists far beyond our conscious level. We shortchange ourselves in thinking we can't tap into our higher self, the self that was made in the image of God. For most of us that communication is called conscience. For LePar it may go beyond that to a more direct channel, a pipeline direct from the higher self to the conscious mind. Or, for reasons to be explained, it may be from a source at the very feet of God.

And here is where the ability to willingly suspend your disbelief is rigorously challenged. For some of the information you are about to read does indeed come from the very portico of God's house. (Remember all the while that if you do not accept this concept, if you think it is all nonsense, that is fine. Set such an idea aside. The information stands up well on its own merits.) I don't know from what level the majority of LePar's information is derived. All I know is that he "hears" it spoken to him while he is conscious of what is going on. He hears it and passes it on. That is the information from which these essays have come. It is very nearly a literal transcription from the spiritual. But behind the little essays, and one might say at the core of all of them, is a vast tome of knowledge whose source I do know. It forms the moral and spiritual base of all these essays. It comes from a source that claims to be but one step away from co-existence with God. It comes from The Council, a group of souls whose final step in spiritual growth is to share knowledge with mankind. It's not for me to try to convince you that The Council exists. I have heard them speak through LePar as he lay in an unconscious state, allowing them to use his body to speak directly to a group of people in the room. You will find The Council mentioned often in these essays. They have provided the moral heart of LePar's ideas. I will forbear saying anything further about The Council—the reader can form his own opinion about such a radical concept when he encounters their quotes in the text. Besides, I am hardly qualified to try to explain the existence of spirits so far advanced above those of us on the physical plane.

Earlier I mentioned a few of the big names of Western literature. Yet, I wouldn't want the reader to assume that I am making any comparisons with this book on literary merit. My purpose was strictly to present the idea of influence from the spiritual realms. Indeed little thought was given by the author as to style and polish. The purpose of this book was not to create a masterpiece of style, but to directly communicate ideas about spirituality, morality, and how to keep them a part of our lives. You may find the phrasing wildly inconsistent—at times very simple and easy to understand, at other times quite indirect and almost tortured. Much to the consternation of the editor, the author insisted on not smoothing some bumpy sections. If you find yourself re-reading such passages you will have discovered why. By forcing you to stop in perplexity as to what the author meant, he has induced you to stop and think for yourself—if you are not quite sure what the author had in mind it makes you use your own mind. It's similar to poetry. Most good poems are somewhat obscure—the reader must expend some energy and bring something of himself to the poem to figure it out.

It could be of some help in understanding the concepts presented in this book to know a little bit about the author. To say that he is a psychic and mystic is to take a chance on alienating the more spiritually conservative readers. Again, accept that concept if you can, but if not, just believe that he is a sincere Christian of high moral character, for he is that too. The titles of Christian and psychic are not necessarily mutually exclusive, if you can agree that even a Christian can be in contact with the spiritual world. After all, isn't that why we pray?

Bill has been aware of a psychic "knowing" since earliest childhood. Indeed he cannot remember a time when he didn't have "the second sight." As a youth he was able to foresee future family events, including tragedies. As might be expected, the foretelling of dire family happenings was not too popular. He resolved to discourage his psychic abilities, and lead the normal life of his peers. He was successful at this, for a while. He settled down, secured employment as a steelworker, and married, never telling anyone of his latent psychic powers.

But it was not to last. A higher calling awaited him, and it was not to be denied. He was fortunate to meet a mentor, Ruth, who was able to show him how his psychic abilities could be controlled. More importantly, she helped him to see that it was not necessary to avoid them if the decision was made that they would be used only for good. Her tutoring enabled him to become comfortable with his gift, to reconcile it with his traditionally strict Catholic beliefs. It also helped to prepare him to accept the most important step in his life—contact with The Council.

It has been Bill's great fortune to know exactly what his purpose is on earth. (Bill would be quick to point out that it is a great burden as well, for all personal interests must be subdued to the higher purpose.) His whole life had been a preparation for the transmission of spiritual insights and moral direction from a higher spiritual plane, a plane whose inhabitants care deeply about us, who love us with a love that we cannot even imagine. What greater calling could a human have than to be the conduit for communication from heaven to earth? And so we have this book. One could say that it is no great accomplishment to write a book from psychic impressions, that there is no "writing" involved at all. On the other hand one could say that he has spent his whole life in the writing.

One final note. Throughout the book you will find quotes from The Council interspersed among the essays. They have been set in the form of poetry, though they were not actually given to us as poems. Yet they have the "feel" of poetry—succinctness of thought and beauty of line, and so they were given that form. Also, the epigraphs were written by Mr. LePar but not in conjunction with the essays themselves. So if they do not match perfectly with the thoughts within the essays, it is not the author's fault, but the editor's who selected them. The combination of essays, poems, and epigraphs are in keeping with the title *Spiritual Harvest*. We hope you find it spiritually bountiful.

THE EDITOR

Just as we are drawn to the light of God,
as moths to a flame, so is God drawn
to where love is, as a moth to a flame.

Chapter 1

The Moth to the Flame

Since the beginning of mankind, we have always been drawn naturally to a light, whether it be a physical light or the light of some lost remembrance of a greater state. See how the butterfly is drawn to the light of a beautiful flower. Once landing on its petals, bathed in the reflective glow of its brilliant host, it is served the sweet nectar that is the sustenance of its life. We who are more like the moth, traveling in a land of darkness, instantaneously are attracted by the distant glow. We seek that brilliant light so that it may illuminate the darkness through which we must travel. We seek that warmth so that it may comfort us in our flight.

Is it not so that the light is provided as an act of love to guide us to a safer place? Is it not an act of love that the light provides us with a warmth? Is it not an act of love that the light illuminates the dark place in which we flutter? Is it by accident that man's conception of light is the symbol for the Giver of all that is necessary and meaningful to man? Have we not realized yet that there are no such things as accidents? That certain symbols, certain concepts, are a part of our inner being, our outer reality, so that that Love that is represented by the Light is always before us, if we choose to see it, if we choose to accept it? Is it possible that we can even begin to conceive of the light, of the flame, if there were not at least a modicum of love within us?

If there is even a small spark of love within us, then the ultimate is unavoidable. It is only a matter of time before that spark of love is drawn back into the original Source of that love. Regardless of how far distantly removed that spark has become the spark and the source are of a oneness, thus they must be drawn and once again united. And if that spark is lost in despair and darkness, then the truth will reign in this: that the Source of the light will also reach out to that spark in the distance.

Do these things just happen? Coincidence? No, like will be drawn to like because the whole cannot be whole unless all parts are present. The light cannot be as brilliant as its greatest potential if one spark is absent. The spark itself, lost in its situation, calls out for help, calls out for reuniting with its whole. Man can fight that natural urge to be drawn to his God, but it is to no avail because he was conceived in love, therefore the love of God is present in him whether he chooses to utilize it or not. This being fact then it is also fact that God will be drawn to him as he is drawn to his Maker.

What is the impelling force of these actions? Nothing short of love. The same love that we can have for each other. The love that we have for each other is the same love that the Divine has for us as individuals. The inescapable fate of man: the uniting of his soul with the Great Soul of His Creator.

Everything in life or creation, whether it is the material aspects or spiritual aspects, is connected. Nothing is isolated. In this fact of reality, that all things are connected, there are bridges or pathways or avenues, which unite all of creation, that we can travel that can bring us to different points or opportunities. Some of these avenues are simple little actions or thoughts, attitudes, or frames of mind. These are for us to use. These are not necessary for the Divine. They are necessary for us. To reach the point of having these attitudes or approaches, we have to achieve a specific understanding, a specific insight, a specific awareness, and the faith to trust in such a child-like action and belief. Remember, it is the child that the Divine encompasses in His Arms and will hold to His Bosom. The rays of God's love reach out to the simple little actions or thoughts or attitudes that carry that small spark of light from ourselves. And as the rays of God's Love connect with us through those simple little actions that we are responsible for, they act as a magnetic draw that levels out our path towards Him. And in this symbiotic connection man is carried to his crowning glory.

The only key to growth,
Spiritual growth,
Is love.
The only action
To spiritual growth
Is love.
The only way or effort
To spiritual growth,
And at-one-ment with
The Divine Father
Is love.
A simple word,
Yet a word
That encompasses so much,
And so completely,
That even a breath from your lungs
Can be an act of love.
And if this be the case,
Then even your unconscious
Breathing
Can be a minister
Of love and healing.

The person who cannot show his feelings
of kindness, love, and compassion,
condemns himself to show only his cruelty.

Chapter 2

The Process Of Spiritual Awakening

Most of us, since we are inclined to bend to our human nature, are in a constant state of transition, back and forth, back and forth. Spirituality demands the opposite. It demands a steadfastness that is not always in line with our human nature. But since we are basically divine in spiritual nature and made in the image of our Divine Father, we have the ability to pull ourselves from this vacillating state. But first we must realize that we have this weakness.

The first thing that we must begin to believe very deeply in our hearts is that we can make any changes or accomplish anything we wish in dealing with our spiritual growth. There are no restrictions, no limitations. As it is, we go from good to bad or from one degree of spirituality to another, in a constant fluctuating back and forth. Some days we find ourselves full of godly love and other days we find we cannot even be bothered with it. This is natural unless you are one of the rare human beings blessed with a very active divine nature. Unfortunately, too few of us are that blessed. During these times of transition, we find ourselves doing things that bring us above our human nature. At such times then we experience a great inner joy or happiness. For example, when we are able to help someone out who is in need, we get a good feeling about doing that. It makes us well up inside with a good feeling. These are the times, these are the experiences, that we must grab hold of and use to begin to develop our human nature into a more divine nature, into a mirror of the Divine Nature, our Infinite Father. This is the state of transition. To move from this point to a higher spiritual consciousness or higher spiritual state, there are three basic steps that we must employ in our activity or life. They are:

Transformation
Consecration
Dedication

Let us deal with the first step, transformation. The word transformation means a metamorphosis or a change in nature or disposition. When we come upon those times that we find ourselves doing something of benefit for someone else, we must grab hold of that good feeling and use it as a stimulus to encourage us to try such deeds again, not to let the opportunity go by the wayside and bear no fruit within ourselves. That good feeling that wells up inside our chest must be savored until the next opportunity comes along where we can receive the same such feeling in another act of love or charity.

We must realize from the very beginning that this will take a very conscious effort on our part. This is not something that will come very naturally at first to most of us. So we must constantly remind ourselves of the wonderful feeling we received when we did show a measure of love or charity to someone else. We must begin to place in our mind the thought of that feeling. At times we can liken that wonderful feeling to a sense of power, and it is. It is the power of creation, the power of love. We must begin to cultivate the taste for that creative power that love gives us. So in the first steps of transformation, we must begin to savor the joys of creative love and brotherhood and then cultivate a stronger desire for that emulation of the Infinite Father.

Dedication

Transformation is the realization of the joy we receive through the experience of helping someone else either by our words or our deeds. This becomes the foundation for the second step which is dedication. Dedication is giving ourselves totally to an activity or to our quest for spirituality.

In the very beginning of the dedication period, we can expect to go through a period of vacillation such as we did in the transformation period. This is to be expected based on our human nature. Our spirituality can be compared to a muscle in our body that has not been used. At first, it must be carefully and slowly exercised into a stronger and more healthy state. So we must constantly remind ourselves not to become discouraged. We are not yet perfect but we are beginning to work on it. Perfection comes according to the degree of our desire, and the degree of our desire must be cultivated into bloom as one would cultivate a seed into a plantlet, into a plant, and into a blooming flower.

To help in cultivating our desire, we should attempt to associate ourselves with people who are not preaching to us but whose lives show that they are actively involved in helping others and doing for others. This type of person can stimulate our fortitude and our desire to help others.

It might also be helpful to set a goal so that we can gauge our progress. Set three time slots in which to meet progressively more difficult goals. The first time slot is a three-month period in which each week we extend a helping hand in some manner to another individual to such a degree that when we reflect on that act of charity or love we experience an uplifting joy of accomplishment. That may mean in some cases that we need to extend ourselves a number of times until we have that experience that gives us that intense feeling of love or joy.

A point of evaluation of our own activities during this time can be the degree of effort needed on our part to instigate or to be involved in the loving act or deed.

We may choose to repeat to ourselves from time to time during our day, "I have the ability to love as God loves me." If we repeat that from time to time, it may stimulate us to keep our eyes open for the next opportunity. What we are doing in the first three months is developing a good habit of observing people to discover opportunities to help them.

Remember, a godly state is a state of active love, a state of active brotherhood. A remark from the Bible comes to mind: "What you have done to the least of mine, you have done to me." Each time we lend a helping hand, regardless of the manner in which we have done it, we are helping someone. We must practice the effort of extending our hand in a helping manner as opposed to extending our hand in a taking manner, which is our human nature.

An example. We have all been in a hurry at times. Say you are walking down the street and someone stops you to ask if you know the directions to a particular place. Now, you are familiar with the town and you know how to get there, but because you are preoccupied and in a hurry you do not want to take the time to give the individual the complicated directions to the spot they are hunting for. So, you very quickly say, "No, I don't know where it is," and you move on. I am sure we have all found ourselves doing this or something similar at one time or another.

This is an instance where we could do a little giving, where we could be a little more charitable or loving. We never know how important that appointment might be for the other person who needs directions. A simple little act of brotherly love or charity such as this can foster a great deal of love. Most people, when a kindness is shown to them, will remember that kindness and when they have an opportunity will recall that courtesy or kindness that was shown to them and will return that deed in one manner or another.

So change comes about through the constant practice of these little things. It is true that in the beginning we will not be successful every time; we will not constantly be thinking in a spiritual manner, but as we continually practice we begin to develop a loving habit that becomes more frequent, more natural, more active. In the overall picture, as time goes by, it will not be something we always have to think about, it becomes a natural part of our being.

To reiterate, once a week we must experience that intense emotional or spiritual high that we receive from a good deed or an act of brotherly love; that warm, wonderful feeling we get from helping someone.

For the second three-month period we commit ourselves to having that experience twice a week. By the time we get to the third three-month period we are beginning to build up the strength of our spiritual muscles, and, consequently, we find it becomes easier. In this third three-month period we increase our effort to experience three of these spiritual or loving highs.

We continue this process until we are at the point that we are experiencing these elevating or uplifting highs once a day.

We may say to ourselves, "This is a very simple thing to do. This is a very simple process. This isn't all that involved." At a physical and emotional level, this is true, but at a spiritual level a very complex miracle is taking place. What we are actually doing is training our physical and emotional states to be more compatible with our higher spiritual state. In essence we are beginning to build a road or pathway to our higher self or our godly self. The communicator, or carrier, of this spiritual strength is the uplifting highs or spiritual fixes that we have become so fond of experiencing. We are educating ourselves in the act of clear channeling from our higher self, that is, allowing our godliness to descend to its heavier form and expression, the physical body and the material world we live in.

Sometimes it is wise for us to look upon spiritual evolvement as a very simple process; that is to deal with things that are more akin to our basic awareness without becoming too involved with the immense complex activities of our spiritual self, or our higher self. Let that be revealed to our selves as our higher self deems proper.

If we follow these suggestions we can transcend the complexities and sometimes contradictive thoughts and opinions of exterior influences such as philosophies and man's interpretation of Divine Law.

I am not saying that we should disassociate ourselves from spiritual religious philosophies, but that these philosophies relate to us according to our state of existence. In that respect they are essential as a support system and essential in stimulating us into an attitude of brotherly love, which is the foundation of all spirituality and creation.

Let us look at spiritual love and brotherly love as a virus. Make it our desire to infect and affect all of mankind with love.

Consecration

In the first step, the process of transformation, we learn that we can make changes and accomplish anything we choose. In this first step we realize that we have a spiritual muscle that has atrophied. In the second step, dedication, we learn that perfection comes according to the degree of our desire. In this step through the art of practicing, we become more fully aware of this atrophied spiritual muscle, and we begin to work a strength back into this spiritual muscle.

In the process of spiritual awakening, the final step, consecration, can be likened to the capstone atop the pyramid of spiritual awareness. It is taking this spiritual muscle and making it a part of our total awareness. One could say that the third step, consecration, is the combination of the first two steps. Consecration is the sum total of the efforts involved in the emulation of deity. It is developing a degree of awareness: first, the awareness of the limits that we allow our human nature to place on us; second, the greater awareness of our ability to change those limitations, expand them beyond our wildest dreams.

In consecration, we deliberately and willfully extend our holiness or godliness through the awareness factor of love. Through the practice of the second step of dedication we have established an avenue of outer activity that could only have been sustained through an inner awareness that is originally a part of our truer or higher being. We must be willing, as an essential part of the third step, consecration, to accept the fact that the total purpose of our expression is the outward manifestation of love: this means action on our part. This action of love cannot be limited to speaking about love but must first be expressed in activities that project out from us or flow out from us to others.

Let us go back to a verse that we used in dedication and bring it to a more personal level. "What you have done to the least of mine, you have done to me." Now is the time that we put this verse or statement in a personal context. We apply it directly to ourselves. We take the position of a christ, a son of God, an anointed chosen one: what we have done for those around us, those less fortunate, after all is said and done, we have ultimately done for ourselves.

We are to look at those around us as extensions of ourselves; we are related by a much greater bond than blood. That bond is the spiritual bond, the spiritual relationship. When parents conceive children, they find an extension of themselves in that new life, not only physically but emotionally. In bringing love to an activity that is directed to others we are filling a segment of a circle so that it ultimately returns back to the source of its origin, namely ourselves. In this activity we too then find extensions of ourselves. In this process of return, the amount of love that we originally sent out begins to attract more of that power, so that when it returns to its seat of origin, it has been multiplied many times over. As it returns to us then we are enriched by the amount that it has been multiplied.

Each soul, each entity, that was ever created is an individual point on a circle. Those individual points must be connected to one another by the divine flow of love. Those souls or entities or individuals that for one reason or another have been excluded from compassion or love have not been allowed to be productive entities in this divine in-flow of creation. In consecration we exercise our awareness of this circle of love and in this we then pour forth our energies in hope that all are connected to one another. The interlocking circles, the symbol for eternity which sometimes is used in reference to a marriage, symbolize the unending relationship that each of us has with one another. Consecration is the acceptance of our ability to express divine love and, in our concern for others, to allow it to flow from within to those in need of compassion and under-standing, to those in need of an outstretched hand of giving.

In God's ways
There is no such thing as instant,
And yet in God's ways
All things are now.
Allow God to utilize the creation;
Allow Christ to bring healing
On many levels in natural ways;
Allow Christ to heal
That which you cannot see,
And that which you can never know
About another soul
Or a human being.

There are no new Truths,
only new ways to declare them.

Chapter 3

Ancient Wisdom to Spiritual Growth

How many times have you heard that a lecture or a book would reveal to you ancient mysteries or ancient secrets of spiritual growth, yet you come away wondering if possibly you hadn't missed something? You were no more aware of a mystery or a secret than you were before you read the book or attended the lecture. Is it possible that in actuality no such information was really given, but instead what was printed or spoken was a grandiose presentation of verbiage? Many of us who have been on a sincere search for spiritual growth have found ourselves in such positions, and over many years of dealing with spirituality, I finally realized that there are no ancient secrets or lost wisdoms or ancient mysteries concerning the road to spiritual growth. All this information for spiritual growth and evolvement that supposedly was lost or kept secret for only a few special individuals has never really existed in a form that was held by a select few.

Wouldn't it be astounding to realize that these supposed ancient secret mysteries concerning spiritual growth or evolvement have been before our very noses all along? Wouldn't it be amazing if someday we were to come upon a plan for spiritual growth that has been before our very eyes since man has been able to record the hours, the days, the months, and the years of his existence?

I have come to realize that there are many ways that the Infinite Father has revealed to us the proper path to spiritual evolvement, our re-uniting with Him, and I would like to share with you one of these Divinely constructed paths of spiritual growth.

Have you ever noticed how the religious calendar of events seems to parallel the growth cycle of nature or the seasonal cycle of a year? After the festive events of the New Year, we go into a time of relative inactivity. The winter months have a natural tendency to slow down our activities and keep us a little closer to the home fires and the season then gradually moves to the next festive occasion of the religious calendar which is, of course, Easter, the universal symbol of resurrection.

The seasonal cycle of the year is like the progression of man's spiritual growth. In the winter months of the first part of the year, nature affords us the opportunity to stick closer to the home fires because of the lack of activities. We are given a time to contemplate our life and what we have done with it and our attitudes toward life and those individuals we must deal with. Unfortunately, too many of us do not use the opportunity for recollection and self evaluation that we have at this time of the year. Instead we indulge ourselves in more time spent in front of the television set. I wonder how much more productive our lives would become if we took the time to contemplate our day? Say you were to take 15 or 20 minutes a day and sit down somewhere in silence and just think about what you have done during the day, and how you have dealt with different experiences involving other people during that day.

Let us take a cue from nature and her cycles. During the cold winter months, plants and some animals go into what appears to be a state of dormancy. In actuality the plants and animals continue to undergo some sort of growth process, as they prepare for the re-emergence of the manifestation of the productivity of life which will eventually lead to the bearing of fruit and the harvest. By taking an inward journey of reflection and evaluation of our own state, we can come face to face with those attitudes that may need changing. At times looking at a true reflection of ourselves can prove painful, but isn't it better to experience this temporary inner discomfort than to allow such conditions to continue, bringing us a far greater discomfort from their outer manifestations? Also, there is the potential of finding ourselves having no control over the time or the intensity of the resulting pain caused by such activities or attitudes. We do not live in an isolated existence but are part of an all-encompassing picture. We have only so much control over our own sphere of experiences. So while we are in this season of quietness and lessened activity, let us utilize it to its greatest possible potential. Let us welcome the opportunity it offers for insights into ourselves, bringing a new awakening, which it was originally intended to do.

As the religious seasons of man and the seasons of nature move on hand in hand, we come to the time of the eve of the Resurrection and spring. The eve of the Resurrection is the Lenten season. The inner season corresponding to the Lenten season is our realization of the weaknesses that lie within each of us and our willingness to accept those weaknesses and initiate the necessary effort to correct those weaknesses, as much as we are able to, according to our own individual strengths. The momentum created in the effort to change ourselves to a more godly individual opens up a floodgate of Divine Grace or Divine Strength that carries us over to that time that the calendar refers to as the Resurrection. Each step of spiritual growth that we can establish in our individual character makes of us a new person. Consequently, we can say we are resurrected into a being more glorious than what we were before. In a sense we can say there has been a new evolvement of Christ Consciousness in us. We have come to our own personal unique resurrection wearing robes of glory according to our individual abilities and desires to change.

This brings us to the springtime then of our own personal evolvement. In the springtime the dormancy of nature breaks forth into the seeds of new life. With these new facets of change added to our character, the spring of our inner seasons offers us the chance to learn the practice of this new awareness in whatever opportunities life may show to us. But, as does a child, we must learn to develop a strength so that we have the stamina to exercise this new awareness of ourselves in the face of family, friends, or world that may be hostile to a more loving person. All the faults that we discover within ourselves, regardless of how they may manifest themselves, ultimately can be reduced to the main stumbling block in spiritual growth and that is the inability to practice an unconditional brotherly love for ourselves and all those with whom we come into contact.

What do I mean by an unconditional brotherly love for ourselves? Far too many people do not really like themselves, let alone love themselves. Many people will make positive statements about themselves, yet they don't really believe what they are saying. There is a hollowness and shallowness in their words. It is as if by trying to convince others they wish to convince themselves. This is impossible. This lack of self-esteem or self-brotherly love is a natural weakness in each of us. This self-brotherly love or self-esteem must first come from that inner awareness inside of us and then emanate from the inner to the outer.

You must love yourself not in an egotistical or self-serving way but in a respectful way. You must care for yourself enough, you must love yourself enough, to raise yourself above attitudes and actions that demean your very being. I am not talking about an egotistical attitude about yourself. I am not saying that you should feel superior to someone else. You must be willing to stand in your proper place and be willing to serve those who need what you may have. You must be willing to give of yourself to the needs of others. You must be willing to accept the potential responsibility that a kindly smile or a pat on the back may be the very factor that will help someone in an hour of need. Taking that extra moment, making that extra effort to look beyond ourselves and our own situation to our neighbor's need or situation may someday mean as much to us and our growth and realization as it may mean to the person we are helping at that moment.

We oftentimes hear that each of us has a spiritual mission to fulfill. This is true. Each of us has a grand, grand mission in life. Is it to lead a group of one hundred, two hundred, two thousand people to enlightenment? No, that is just a person who is capable of being a catalyst for an activity. The real great or grand missions in life are those everyday occasions that we encounter wherein we recognize the worth and value of another individual. If there is such a thing as a mystery or a secret, it is this: We cannot love or respect another individual unless we know what love and respect is, and if we do not have that love and respect for ourselves, then we are not capable of recognizing it outside of ourselves. If we are not capable of seeing the godly potential in ourselves, then we are not capable of realizing that godly potential in another individual, in our brother or sister.

This Divine Creator can see His own Godliness and He can see the godliness that lies in each of us. If we in turn are to emulate Him, we must first be able to see our own potential or godliness before we are able to see it in anyone or anything else in creation. I tell you now that this Divine God has not and will not create anything that does not have the full potential of goodness and perfection. Only we are capable of allowing the power of the Divine to flow through us, cleansing away the cobwebs of inactivity and shining outwardly to the world. At this time in man's history the Divine Creator manifests Himself and reveals Himself more completely to His creation through each of us as unique individuals. Therefore, it is not only our right but privilege to be His personal ambassador to all. We must choose to stand before Him and allow His radiance to pass through us to those beyond, thus allowing this light to eliminate all shadows that we may cast upon His creation. We must be willing to stand completely transparent in the full view of our Creator.

So in spring then we must resurrect the new-born babe from our old self, and during this time of infant maturation we make preparation for the fullness that is to follow. We timidly venture forth, as a small child would, testing ourselves and building strength.

As this continues through the seasonal cycle of nature and our own inner cycle we reach the stage of maturing, summer. Here in this season we confidently practice our new awareness of Divine Love, not fully realizing that these efforts continue to develop an extended part of our own being that we are prevented from seeing. Although at times our efforts may be difficult, yet we are carried forth by the momentum of these changes and efforts within us. The purpose of this hidden aspect is to ensure that our continuation of growth is motivated by an undaunted spiritual love for ourselves and all around us. To have a true spiritual or brotherly love for others we must first have enough respect and self-esteem for ourselves so that we WILL truly love ourselves as a child and heir of God. This is the cornerstone of any and all spiritual growth in the emulation of the Christ.

In nature fall is the season of the harvest and maturity. All through the summer the plants matured and gained strength creating secret treasures under their rich, green leaves. We, too, in our entrance into the time of harvest have done the same thing. During our summer season, during this season of unconditional love, a beautiful treasure has been hidden from our eyes. In our time of harvest we are then permitted to see the bounty of fruit that has been kept secret from us. This chest of treasure that has developed through our loving activities is now ours, to nourish us and to bring us even greater fulfillment. This is the harvest; these are the fruits of our labor; this is the sustenance that is permanently ours and can never be taken away. All the love, the kindness, the consideration that we have shown others is permanently returned to us in the form of a golden step in our climb to a oneness with the Infinite Father.

As the season continues, winter again approaches according to nature's cycle and our time of rest is with us. Corresponding to nature in the calendar of man's religions, the season of Christ's birth approaches. In our personal growth cycle the innocence of a newborn babe is reestablished within our own being. We must then allow this innocent child, which is the truth that is innate within us all, to manifest itself in us and show us those things that must be changed. We must be willing to accept that manifestation as another step of spiritual evolvement. So again the seasons of nature continue over a familiar path of proven growth. The inner cycle of spiritual growth of each man also begins again: the unavoidable destiny, the "godification" of our being.

You cannot dream dreams of spirituality
While the world passes you by.
    This
Is your framework of growth;
    This
Is your framework of doing.
Read your books on spirituality;
Dream your dreams of spirituality,
But they are for naught
Unless you are willing
To actively do something
With yourself.
The Divine Essence
Has given you all a time now
Where you can make
Great spiritual growth
So easily,
And it is beyond our understanding
Why you cannot take advantage of it.

God does not deprive the soul
of anything it needs.
God gives in abundance and more.

Chapter 4

Turning the Karmic Cheek

With a diligent search of the world's scriptures, one will always find a reference to turning the other cheek. In our society today we find that many people consider this a sign of cowardice or weakness. Yet for the initiate, it is a sign of great spiritual strength, insight, and knowledge. One may ask, how can this be? One should ask, (where karma is concerned) how could this not be?

Let's say you move into a new neighborhood and you strike up an acquaintance with the people next door. As soon as you move into your house, they come over and introduce themselves. Immediately, you develop a sense of rapport with them. A few days later, the neighbors in back of you come over and introduce themselves, but there is a distance or a coldness that seems to exist. There is not the warmth that there was with the family next door. As time goes on a greater gulf of coldness develops between you and the neighbor behind you. This coldness does not develop because of anything instigated by you and your family but comes about because of the nature of your humanness and their humanness. In other words, the personalities involved just do not mesh harmoniously. Over a period of time the neighbors in back begin to imagine that you have been deliberately cold towards them, and this hostile attitude grows even greater as they see a deeper friendship begin to develop between you and the family next door. The family in back of you become jealous as they see this friendship begin to flourish. Out of this jealousy then those neighbors behind you begin to make small innuendoes and slurs about you and your family to some of the other neighbors. As the jealousy grows even greater in the neighbors behind you, the slurs and innuendoes turn into damaging lies about you and your family.

Do you defend yourself and family by explaining away the rumors? This is a spiritual crossroads. In most cases our human nature would dictate striking back. Fight fire with fire. But here is a great opportunity to rise above our human nature and fight that fire with a quenching bucket of ice cold water. What is this water that we use? It is this: do nothing. Do not defend yourself against the lies. Place your defense in the hands of our Divine Source, our God, ask Him to protect you from the ravages of such lies. How great can our defenses be against such stumbling blocks to spirituality in comparison to the defense that this Infinite Source can give in our behalf? Remember, He is a Loving Father, and we are His children. If an earthly father would go to any lengths to protect his child from danger, think how much further our Heavenly Father would go to protect us and defend us from danger.

With this action, what have we actually done? First, we have placed our protection from our adversaries in the hands of a far greater defender than we could ever hope to be. This means that our enemies must deal with this Protector and not us. Also, in a situation like this our enemies are actually presenting us with an opportunity to develop a karmic situation that we can either accept or reject. By not defending ourselves, we are rejecting the debt and not accepting a possible occasion to stoop to their level of negative activity, that of defaming another individual. It also means that what they sent out will be returned to them in whole, since we did not add to or become a part of a negative action. They threw out the negative boomerang, and it must return then to them. So with this, karma goes home. It returns to its source of origin. Consequently, the negative actions that they perpetrated must be dealt with and answered for in the setting of their relationship between themselves and their Divine Source. They must answer for their trespasses against the outgoing activity of Divine Love. In essence then our neighbors have slapped us on our cheek and we have turned the other cheek and offered it to them. We have refused to accept a negative challenge from them. The negative action that was sent out by them had not been accepted by us, consequently, it must return to them, and they then must deal with it. This leaves us in a state of positive movement. We move ahead and up, away from that which would drag us down or backwards. We have demonstrated our faith in the Divine Presence by leaving our defense in the Hands of our Infinite Father.

In all of existence there are only two motions, forward to the positive or backward towards the negative, towards our Divine Source or backwards away from our Divine Source. In our state of existence there is no such thing as a neutral state, no such thing as standing still. We either grow or regress. In the situation with the neighbors we chose to grow instead of regress. We have chosen to show our strength and our insight by rejecting an invitation to a negative situation. It is true that those neighbors may continue to embarrass us with lies, but we can gain great strength in the knowledge that the more they try to destroy us, the greater the stumbling blocks they are placing in their own path of evolvement, and sooner or later they will have to answer in full for those trespasses. Hopefully, they will see the error of their ways before they incur too great a debt. We have crossed their path in life so that they may have an opportunity to grow with us by sharing in love and respect for each other. As a creation of this Divine Source we are guaranteed the absolute right to total and complete free will choice. It is absolutely essential if we are to be truly made in the image of God. Nothing or no one can force us to move away from our Divine Source. Only we have control of our destiny. Anything less than this makes us puppets and not true, living and god-like entities. We cannot control all of creation, but we can control our own state of existence.

This little example and our response to it is, of course, under ideal conditions. Taking into consideration our humanness and our ego, we do not always act as perfectly as we know we should. Remember that all of us take steps backward from time to time. To recover our original state, we must retrace those steps in some manner to regain the forward motion.

This demonstrates again the great Love of the Infinite Father. He realizes that at times we must learn through our mistakes, so the door on spiritual growth is never closed to us. The opportunity to join hands in at-one-ment with our Divine Creator is never taken away from us. Regardless of what we have done in the past, there is always some way of making correction for it now.

Not even God,
The Almighty Creator,
Has predestined anything for you.
He has bounced you on his knee
And said, "Dear child,
What is it you want to do?"
And then has let you
Go your way and do it.
Oh, it is true,
He will tap you on your shoulder
And either say, "No, no" or "Yes, yes,"
But ultimately it is your choice
To say, "All right, I will listen,"
Or "Sorry old man, I know better."
And how many times have all of you
Done that very thing?
And, in fact, we will say to you,
How many times,
When we were in your situation,
We did that very thing?

God the Father, God the Son,
God the Holy Spirit find their earthly
expressions in life, love, and beauty.

Chapter 5

The Infinite Creator and the Finite Creature

It was a Saturday afternoon in October. As my wife was getting ready to leave the house, she reminded me that later that evening we would have to go into town. She also reminded me that I would have about three hours in which to play at being an artist before she would be back. She gave me a loving peck on the cheek and went flying out the door with the words, "See you later, honey."

At last! The serenity and majestic silence that a great painter needs to express his ability on the canvas before him. I stood there for a moment, staring at the ominous white canvas. Its gigantic size of ten inches by fourteen inches began to overwhelm me with its power. Immediately, I realized I needed fortification to attack this giant. I ran quickly to the nearest coffee pot, filled a large mug with the black liquid of strength, inhaled its sweet aroma, then allowed the rich fluid to slip across my lips and tongue and fill my innards with a fortifying warmth. My courage had been enhanced. I immediately walked to the easel, grabbed the palette, selected a tube of paint, and determinedly squeezed out a glob of color. The mastery with which I achieved this first step gave me the courage to repeat it a number of times more so that my palette had a rainbow of color on it. I grabbed my first weapon of attack—a fine precision instrument—its red-sable bristles were a full quarter-inch wide. Just the instrument needed to turn the stark white canvas into a living creation of beauty. With firm determination, I took the deadly instrument and began to approach the rainbow of color. I gave the white canvas a quick glance and stopped the brush in mid-movement. It then began to dawn on me that I could not think of anything to paint. Would this great artist be halted in midstep by a simple problem of what to fill the canvas with? Not on your life! A moment or two of thought would be all that would be needed to visualize a great picture that could be reproduced on the canvas. A moment went by. Thoughts flashed across my mind at the speed of light, but none stopped. A moment or two went by. A moment or three. A moment or four . . . The great weapon that once was poised for attack drooped sorely in my hand. I guess the great general had met his Waterloo. I dropped forsaken in my chair and looked sadly at the canvas. One of the rare times that I have to myself in which I can pursue one of my great desires in life comes to me, and I cannot think of a thing to paint. Ten minutes go by and I have not touched the canvas.

Time was flying by and I was becoming desperate. I stood up and walked to the window and looked out at the fields behind the house. My eyes followed a young deer that casually walked and then grazed and then walked and then grazed. A beautiful pheasant came swooping down out of the sky and landed close to the back fence. It pecked here and there in the weeds, moved a little farther in this direction, pecked some more, and then moved in some other direction, and pecked more. Three rabbits merrily chased each other near the fence post. They enjoyed the warm sun as they played hide and seek or some form of "rabbit tag" with each other. A bluebird landed on the fence post, playing sentinel for the rabbits. And when his tour of duty had finished, a robin took over the chores. My eyes moved to the old oak tree at the far end of the field. Its leaves were beginning to darken with the fall color. Its massive trunk gave way to Herculean arms that spread up and held the crown of darkening leaves.

I marveled at the beauty that our Creator paints for us every day of our lives. If we could only see this beauty more often, instead of blinding ourselves to it . . . We as humans try so hard to create beauty only from ourselves.

A thought crossed my mind: Those things, events and people that are truly beautiful in life, we begin to see on closer observation, have their beauty because they are reflecting the Divine Creator Himself. I walked back to the blank canvas and thought to myself, "How can any man hope to create a truly beautiful piece of art? He can only hope to hold the paintbrush for the Divine Creator."

The poor are there for a reason.
They are there to help those
Who need help in growth.
Do not lose a great opportunity to grow.
Whatever you give will most assuredly
Be returned to you.
That is a fact of creation,
Because by giving you are creating,
And what you create
You will have to face,
And it will become a part of you.
So, when you reach down
To help someone in need,
You are creating something positive,
And that is what will be
In your future to deal with,
To have,
To become a part of.

*We condemn ourselves to learning
more from adversity than from happiness.*

Chapter 6

Guilt: The Destroyer
or Builder

One evening as I was talking with a small group the subject of guilt came up. One of the individuals at our gathering said he was receiving some counseling and that during one of the sessions his counselor stated, "There is no fault or guilt, only consequences or circumstances." The individual wanted to know what The Council had to say with regard to this topic.

I asked him what his personal opinion was concerning such a statement. He felt that it was a healthy attitude to have because it freed you from constraints. My reply to him was, "Your observations are very accurate. But that is the problem with such concepts or philosophies or attitudes."

With an attitude such as this what you are really saying is that it is absolutely all right to do anything you please as long as you are not caught. You are saying we shouldn't feel any guilt or there shouldn't be any fault that we must assume unless we get caught and have to face the consequences.

A few years ago in California a man went into a McDonalds with an automatic weapon and began shooting, killing a number of women, children, and men. An extreme example, certainly, but how would you feel if it had been your child or some other member of your family that had been murdered? Would you still feel that this concept is a healthy concept or a proper concept? Hardly. To say the very least, you would be outraged. You would want that individual to pay the maximum for such outrageous conduct.

Would you really be able to say that the death of your child or the death of a member of your family was simply the consequences of an individual's action? Or would you be able to say it was not that individual's fault, it was simply the circumstances involved? No, you would not have any of these attitudes. Your heart would be racked with pain. Your eyes would be swollen and red from the tears that you shed. And you would be screaming that this animal be brought to justice.

Many of the self-help groups and support groups use this no-fault philosophy, but there is a danger in it, a very serious danger.

This type of concept says to us, directly or indirectly, that it is perfectly all right to do anything that you choose to do as long as you do not get caught or you are willing to pay the consequences if you do get caught. It also implies that it is all right to do what you choose to do because the circumstances may have prompted you into such action.

In actuality, this eliminates personal responsibility for ourselves and our actions. These attitudes give us carte blanche to do whatever we please for whatever reason we feel we have justification. I would hope that these support groups that dispense such advice are insuring that the individual being counseled understands completely the context in which it is meant.

If a member of our family is an alcoholic or drug user, many times we may feel that we are responsible for this. In these situations, we must realize that it is not our fault nor should we bear any guilt feeling. The problem lies directly with the individual who may be addicted, whether it is drugs, alcohol or even wife-beating. It is not directly our fault. It is true that in some situations individuals involved in such dilemmas can be considered codependents. This is because they assume the responsibility for the actions of the other person, and in so doing they feel that they are at fault or they are guilty. In a situation such as this, we are not to bear the fault or guilt, but we will in part bear the consequences of the situation. This casts an entirely different light on the concept. There is no fault or guilt, only consequences or circumstances. These individuals find themselves not only paying the consequences of the other person's actions, but also find themselves paying for a set of circumstances that may be inescapable.

But in the wider society outside the co-dependent situation guilt plays a different role. It is not all right to do what we may choose to do, just because we are willing to accept the consequences of those actions or that the conditions may allow us to do whatever we choose. Some people feel if I choose to take a handful of pencils or one pencil from work, it is all right as long as the boss doesn't catch me. We must seriously consider people with such attitudes. If they experience no guilt from stealing, quite possibly their next self-centered act may be much more serious.

An individual that does not experience guilt is an individual that is self-serving and self-centered. To what extent an individual like this will go will be determined by how self-serving and self-centered they are. The more self-serving and self-centered an individual is, the less guilt they will experience, therefore the less constraint they will have, the less control they will have over themselves.

Guilt is a very important emotion that is necessary for full spiritual growth or awareness. Guilt is not something that we should run from. It is a tool that can most assuredly further our quest for the God that we believe in.

I would like to share with you a short quote from The Council concerning guilt.

"Do not allow guilt to destroy you because it was never meant to destroy but it was meant to create. Guilt, if handled in a proper way, is an extremely healthy thing, but, unfortunately for mankind, he turns a beautiful gift of God into something that destroys and annihilates the soul. Guilt is the finger pointing to the proper way. Man should learn to accept that direction that the finger is pointing to, and then learn to accept those sets of experiences or circumstances that brought about the finger of guilt."

There is a purpose for this feeling of guilt that some of us experience. Guilt was not intended to destroy us. Its purpose is to create. We experience guilt when we know that we have been responsible for something that has been harmful to ourselves or to others.

Guilt, if used properly, can create in us a caution against further detrimental actions. In this sense, it can be an extremely healthy thing for us, certainly spiritually and in many cases physically.

The Council says that guilt is a beautiful gift from our Creator. Unfortunately, many people allow themselves to be overwhelmed by guilt, thereby making it a destructive element in their personality and a deterrent to future happiness. Every man, woman, and child on the face of the earth, at least at one time in his life, has done something that has caused him to experience the pangs of guilt. Most people realize that this is a signal from some higher element or aspect of our nature that tells us we have been responsible for something that is not good for us, whether it be physically, emotionally, or spiritually. It is something that is contrary to our higher nature. If we utilize guilt as a constructive, creative gift, it is necessary to look at it as a signpost that indicates a direction of travel. As The Council puts it, it is a pointing finger. It shows us where not to go again. It indicates that some other direction should be taken.

Many people have been crushed or destroyed emotionally because of the guilt that they feel. This is definitely an unhealthy state that they have allowed themselves to be put into or to hang on to. Rarely in life are we able to change the past. But there is always the present and the tomorrow that we can work in, that we must work in.

I often recall a statement made by Jesus. He said, "He who is without sin cast the first stone." This statement was made in the context of a little scenario where a woman who was considered a prostitute was to be stoned to death since that was the punishment by law. Not one of those individuals with a clear conscience could throw the first stone. Jesus sent them on their way. It was the guilt that lay within each that prevented them from casting their stones. They were dismissed, to go about their way. These people were forced, with a simple sentence, to face up to the responsibilities of their own guilt. They were prevented from becoming involved in a situation that would bring them even greater guilt and serious consequences. Many of these men knew for a fact that this woman was guilty of prostitution because they themselves had used the woman. Publicly, they carried a contempt for the woman. This contempt was definitely based on their own personal guilt concerning their involvement with the woman. When Jesus challenged them with His statement, He literally forced them to admit to themselves the responsibility and guilt that they carried, thereby giving them the opportunity to face it, accept it, and carry on with the rest of their lives. If we are truly guilty of something, we can turn that emotion into a very productive growth lesson. We must be willing to assume the responsibility for our actions and our deeds, realize the injustice or lack of love involved, and take steps to correct that attitude in us. Guilt becomes destructive only when we refuse to learn from it and move beyond it. Guilt can be a great motivator to more productive and positive elements in our nature or in our life. We should never be so out of control of our situation that circumstances will manipulate us into activities that present guilt as the consequence of those activities. Some individuals will allow guilt to overshadow them to such an extent that they become dysfunctional, thereby relieving themselves, so they think, of the responsibility of change. Guilt, if used properly, is a pointing finger to a more productive tomorrow. Guilt prevents us from traveling over rocky roads, previously traveled, in our quest for our God. Guilt, looked at in a proper light, can set us free from an old and destructive path. It can lead us to a path of enlightenment and happiness.

A hungry man
Hears no talk of spirituality;
What he hears
Is his stomach growling.
Silence that and he will hear other things,
But nine times out of ten you will not
Have to talk to him about spirituality,
He will already have seen it
In your godly actions.
Your actions will have taught him
The activities of God,
Not your words, not your thoughts.
And yet in all this,
Those who give will always end up
With more than what they started out with.
It is a Divine Law, a Divine Principle,
And even the greed and hate of mankind
Will never move one word of that Law,
Never even move it one centimeter.

Only the honest will believe the sincere.
All others are too shallow.

Chapter 7

The Superficial
Seeker

Many people want to know whether they should follow a certain philosophy, or if a concept or philosophy is in fact legitimate. There was a particular woman who had a friend that she was concerned about. This friend of hers became involved in a certain philosophy that a psychic was preaching. To the woman the philosophy just did not seem to ring true, yet there was no way that she could convince her friend that she should be a little more discerning and cautious. According to this particular woman, the philosophy had all the elements that her friend liked to hear. Basically, the philosophy stated in very clever and subtle terms that it was perfectly all right to continue in your present attitudes as long as you continually followed the concepts of this psychic.

A little further investigation into the situation made it quite apparent that this particular woman who was involved with the psychic had very little knowledge of spiritual principles and how they should be applied to life. The sum total of her knowledge was only a superficial understanding, at very best, of her own traditional religious beliefs and upbringing. Looking over the list of psychic and metaphysical books this woman had read, it was quite apparent that she had ingested nothing more than the commercial drivel that abounds in our present-day market, the type of information that only feeds the self-indulgent attitudes so prevalent in our society today. It was very obvious that the woman was totally oblivious to the fundamental principle of spirituality and spiritual growth, that is, being able to control or practice a modicum of self-discipline or control over one's self. The attitude of today's society is to gain all the material possessions that we want, according to our whims, regardless of the future cost to ourselves, society, the environment, and health of our planet.

A close observation of the popular psychics, gurus, channelers, and recognized ministers and televangelists of our day, reveals that their basic themes are: You can have or do anything you want, regardless of how selfish or inconsiderate it may be, as long as you can intellectually convince yourself that it is in your best spiritual interests; or that possessions are the rewards for your spiritual seeking.

Today this is not an unusual situation in the metaphysical field and in the field of orthodox religion. Far too many psychic/guru/channelers are telling the people only what they want to hear so that their own personal fame and wealth is secure.

Just because a psychic has national fame or is able to advertise the availability of his tapes, books, and videos in slick magazines does not indicate his sincerity or honesty in what he is doing. This could very well be a deliberate sham or fraudulent activity to give him power, wealth, and fame.

Good common sense dictates that it is not wise to follow an individual or to base our entire life on what one individual might profess to believe without seriously investigating the individual's background in regard to his personal integrity and lifestyle. All of us are searching for a way of life that will give us purpose and meaning. This makes us vulnerable to those individuals or organizations that have no scruples, that would take advantage of our sincere desire to better ourselves.

We are all attempting to return to our higher state. We are attempting to find ourselves. Yet very few people truly believe that they have anything worthwhile deep within them. Most people do not love themselves in a godly manner. We must remember that we are all children of The God, and, as such, we are made in His Likeness and Image in relationship to our spiritual potentials and qualities.

Loving yourself in a godly manner or having self-respect must be differentiated from a self-serving love. Very few of us wish to delve within ourselves and seek out those higher qualities that are in all of us. Many of us avoid this inward search because of the fear of what we might not find within. Therefore, these people allow the psychics to decide what their potentials are or what they should be in life as opposed to what their true potential is.

We must remember that the ultimate experience in life is to find or express our true selves, the godly nature in us. We cannot find ourselves by following a preacher, a psychic, a guru, or a channeler. We become lost in these so-called leaders. We are not able to find ourselves because of their overpowering charisma or personality.

The Council's information does not preach to us on how to live our lives. The Council prefers to remind us and reawaken us to the tremendous potential within each of us.

We must remember that we are unique. We will never, in the history of the world, be again who we are in this lifetime. We are that magic combination that will never exist again as we do now. Each of us is unique and special. This should bring respect for ourselves. Each has something to give that only we can give. Each has a unique world because of a different perception, a perception that we demonstrate through the most godly and loving ways possible.

The Council says that there is no magic bullet to spirituality and self-awareness. It takes a deliberate willingness to seek out our true being and to manifest it in the world to others.

So what can be done for the woman whose problem introduced this topic? By helping her to think more highly of herself as a unique and special person, she might awaken someday to her own true potential.

Be of a joyful heart,
And a peaceful heart,
And very little frown
Will come to your face.
If the heart sings,
The body cannot cry.

To the man who seeks an explanation for
all spiritual things the soul no longer speaks.

Chapter 8

Long Night of Winter

It is now the end of November. All the lectures and public appearances are finished for this year. For most people winter is a time of rest, when activities slow down. With the exception of the Christmas and New Year holidays, most people's activities are curtailed considerably. The majority of you, when you are finished with your day's work, will return home through the cold and deepening snow, have your dinner, and then retire for the evening, watching television, reading a book, or possibly doing some craft work. For those of you who have a fireplace, some will, on occasion, put a log or two on and sit there and allow the dancing flames of the fire to lull you into a peaceful and tranquil state of mind.

For myself, with the exception of a few rare evenings, it will be necessary to pick a number of topics for lectures in the coming year. These topics will be typed into SOL's computer and for the next day or two, I will watch the electronic brain flicker its numbers and letters across its cyclopean eye and listen to the rhythmic slapping of the printer spitting out hundreds of pages of information. For the next three months it will be necessary to cull the basics of the different subjects from the mountain of paper and then build upon these basic principles with additional information from The Council so that, when it is delivered in a lecture, that information can be utilized in the everyday lives of those who choose to hear.

As I sit here writing, a statement made by The Council some twenty years ago passes through my mind again. The Council said that the information they are giving us is living and that each time we read over that information we will discover that it is saying even more than we realized the first time we read it or the second time or the third time. All great spiritual writings from the past have had a life to them that gives us a greater insight with each reading. They are living and therefore continually instruct us.

I feel a sense of quiet excitement, because even though I think I understand everything The Council has said on a particular subject, as I review that subject, I begin to realize how much more there is to discover in those same passages. As my eyes scan the sentences, the words are devoured by my mind and placed in groups that speak of the meaning, and then as I allow myself to contemplate that meaning, these groupings of words begin to move and reform to render a deeper and more profound understanding. It is much like standing on a mountaintop and shouting a question across the valley, then hearing the echo respond with an answer.

Every time I have this experience, I am overwhelmed with amazement. How could The Council construct such sentences and paragraphs so that with each reading one receives greater and greater nourishment? How fantastically great must their knowledge and wisdom be to be able to interweave so much information with such simple statements? You have already encountered examples of The Council's simple way of teaching. Between each chapter of this book you can find a quotation from The Council set in the form of a poem. You may discover, if you re-read each poem, new insights and meanings that are not obvious at the first reading.

When I was younger, I looked forward to and enjoyed the days of summer. Now that I have become a little older and, it is hoped, a little wiser, I eagerly await and relish the long night of winter. This is the time when I receive my sustenance, my understanding and hope and encouragement from the words of The Council. Going over their words, my mind is refreshed and it is reminded of the simple principles that they speak of, the encouragement and concern they give and have for each one of us.

It is much like a reunion with a beloved family member or a close friend. The comforting and encouraging words of The Council give me the encouragement and the strength to look forward to a new season of lecturing and sharing with old friends and new friends to be.

The long night of winter gives me that needed time to think, to understand, to renew my strength in my quest for spirituality. Just as the winter affords me the opportunity for renewal, it too can be your chance to gain fortification for the coming year. It is your time to allow the words of The Council and other great spiritual writings to inspire you, to give you strength, and rekindle that spiritual light that lies within you. The brighter the spiritual light becomes, the greater the changes we can make in ourselves. The greater the changes we make in ourselves, the greater the changes in those around us and in the world in which we live. May the light of The Christ be rekindled anew in you during your long night of winter.

Your God the Father
Does not punish man.
He is not a two-faced God.
He does not speak of love
And then wield a devastating sword.
He speaks of love,
And He touches gently.
He picks His children up
And holds them to His Bosom
And protects them from themselves,
When He is allowed.

*Those who would see the valley
must rise above the mountain tops.*

Chapter 9

Karma: Real or Just Lip-service?

A few years ago, I was approached by a number of promoters asking me to lend my name to a series of psychic fairs. The individuals involved set forth their proposals to me. I immediately realized that this was purely a mercenary enterprise on their part. As the proposals stood I could not accept them and I offered them alternative proposals which eliminated the tremendous monetary gain and the fraudulent aspects the promoters incorporated into the psychic fair. My proposals would have given the participants more truth of Divine principles and greater value for their time and money. As you may have guessed, this alliance did not come to pass.

There was a moral responsibility to insure that the participants to such events would get a better quality experience at a more reasonable cost. Taking a stand and speaking out publicly about such situations, I knew full well that this stand would not be popular with certain individuals and groups. I was not at all surprised to receive many telephone calls and letters that were extremely nasty, vicious, and threatening. The greatest majority of these letters and phone calls were, as you might suspect, anonymous. The anonymity of these letter writers and callers only encouraged me to speak out all the more. It is my firm belief that individuals like you and me must begin to establish a moral conscience in any aspect of the spiritual field, that is, we must have a moral strength to object to what is not just and true. If I were to have sat quietly in silence, I would have incurred a karmic debt of omission.

We must remember there are two actions in which we can incur a karmic debt: an act of commission and an act of omission. An act of commission is an action taken in some manner, and the act of omission is an action of avoidance, a lack of action, or not being totally truthful.

By speaking out against the injustices I prevented other individuals from drawing me into their karmic debt. This was accomplished by not participating in their activities and by speaking out against such activities that are wrong.

We must remember that karma can also be looked upon as cause and effect. Whatever I may do or not do constitutes the cause. The repercussions or ramifications of the action or lack of action constitutes the effect.

Let me set a scenario to give you an idea of cause and effect. This scenario is actually based on a situation that I was faced with in consulting with a particular woman. She had talked to two other psychics about taking her teenage daughter to a doctor for birth control pills. From their point of understanding, both psychics told her that she would not incur any karma by doing this. Unfortunately for the woman involved, they advised her wrongly.

How does she incur karma from this action? Very simply. First, the mother is condoning promiscuity on the part of the daughter. Second, the mother is adding to the daughter's lack of self-esteem and lack of self-control. Third, it is the obligation of the mother to teach her daughter the proper situation in which to participate in intimate relations, that being, of course, marriage. By assisting the daughter in obtaining birth control pills the mother is also, through her actions, giving her daughter permission to be promiscuous, in essence giving her seal of approval. The mother may very well rationalize her actions by saying, "It is the lesser of two evils. At least she won't become pregnant."

To show how cause and effect work in this situation, let us start with the effect first. The effect is that the daughter with birth control pills is in a position to be as promiscuous as she chooses without the fear of becoming pregnant. In other words, the daughter is in a position to sleep around with as many boys as she wants and as often as she wants. This also opens the door to a wide range of venereal diseases including the dreaded AIDS. If the daughter should contact AIDS and spread this disease to others, this becomes an extending ramification of the unbridled lack of self-control on the part of the daughter that was initially triggered by the mother's permissiveness concerning the birth control pills. The cause then is the mother's permissiveness and cooperation in obtaining the birth control pills for her daughter. Some individuals may argue that it is better to practice birth control than to have an unwanted or illegitimate child. Again, we are faced with permissive rationalization.

The proper situation should have been to teach the children self-respect and self-esteem so they are not using each other for self-indulgent pleasures. Children should be taught that there is a proper time for intimacy and that is under the umbrella of the lifelong commitment of marriage. Anything other than this creates karma. This is a fact, a truth, whether we choose to accept it or not.

If the mother had held her ground, she would not have been drawn into the daughter's karmic situation. Let us go back one step. The mother should have concentrated more strongly on teaching the child self-esteem and self-respect. By being firm and not giving permission to the daughter to use birth control, the mother could add her strength to the daughter in overcoming the promiscuous attitude of today and possibly the peer pressure associated with it. Many times children may use the excuse of "I can't do that. My parents would kill me," to keep from yielding to peer pressure. This helps them to save face with their friends and at the same time to not engage in activities that they really do not wish to participate in.

We must begin to realize that karma is not a stagnant situation or condition. Karma does not stop with just one particular action or inaction. Karma is, in fact, a condition that rolls over upon itself and multiplies in its ramifications. It can be compared to a cascading waterfall where the water falls upon protruding rocks and splashes out in all directions. To avoid karma we must have the moral strength to object to attitudes, conditions, and situations that we know do not add to self-respect, self-esteem, and the character of ourselves and others.

As children of the Light, we must begin to conduct ourselves with the dignity and self-respect of the gods that we are. We must not be afraid to stand up for what we know to be the truth. We must make a decision: Do we truly believe in karma, cause and effect, or is it just so much lip-service?

God does not hide his face from man.
Man hides from God.
Are we gods?
In time, we will be gods.
Are you gods?
Yes, in time you will be gods.
Let us add here at this moment.
Man is not predestined to anything.
He has planned his own life out.
He may reach his ultimate goal
In any way he chooses,
With joy and happiness
Or with pain and sorrow.
There is only one area
That man does not have the free will choice
And that is this:
He is absolutely predestined
To reach his own godhood.
There is nothing that can prevent this.

What we give the earth
the earth gives our children.

Chapter 10

Who's Leading Me
By My Nose Today?

As I looked into the mirror, splashing after-shave lotion on my freshly shaven face, I wondered how long it would be before I would have to worry whether this fragrance was too strong or not. I wondered how absurd our society will become before we finally wake up and begin to take responsibility for our own lives, physically, emotionally, and spiritually.

Some years ago an individual informed me that there was a group of people who were insisting on having areas that were reserved for non-smokers. This particular individual was very happy with the idea and asked for my opinion. I answered that it might be a good idea in some situations to have areas for non-smokers. As these words were coming out of my mouth, I received an intuitive impression: if common sense were applied to the situation, and certain constraints used in order to prevent fanatical or obsessive movements or groups from forming, this would be a perfectly good idea. If such constraints were not initiated in the beginning, it could get so out of control that spin-off groups would begin to demand fragrance-free areas where individuals could not use any fragrances at all.

A few days later during a conversation with another group the subject was brought up again. I decided to share the impression I had received with this group of individuals. I explained to them what I received and cautioned them that if these individuals, in demanding their rights, were not careful, they would eventually infringe upon the rights of others who choose to smoke. Accomplishing this, it would be carried one step further and eventually a group would arise that would demand an area where no one would be allowed to wear any kind of fragrance, such as after-shave lotions, perfumes, scented shampoos, scented underarm deodorants, facial lotions, or body lotions. Some in the group said that that was ridiculous, it would never get that far out of hand.

I simply looked at the group and said, "If this situation is allowed to continue without respectful constraints, you will be surprised how far such fanaticism will go. Don't be surprised if employers will be called upon to divide work areas into smoking, and non-smoking, fragrant and non-fragrant areas."

Again the reaction was that common sense just tells you that it would never get that far out of hand. My reply was, "Don't underestimate the ease with which the public can be swayed and led around by a ring in its nose. Don't be surprised how easily their attention can be drawn from something very serious to something that is nothing more than a distraction from the real problem."

A few weeks ago one of the individuals who sat in on this session called me and reminded me of this psychic impression. The individual told me of a group of individuals in a small community in California that was insisting on a fragrance-free area at the City Council meetings. This small group of individuals pursued their demands to the point that they were allocated an area designated fragrance-free. For a moment I pondered the situation and had to chuckle at how ridiculous people can be, how easily swayed and led they are. Can you imagine in a small room held for City Council meetings a section designated for smokers, a section designated for non-smokers, and a section designated for individuals who wish to protect their nostrils from fragrance? Oh, the absurdity of it all! What next? A section free from people wearing green? Or pink? Or blue?

Then to my further amazement, the following week I received a professional newsletter dedicated to business practices. In this newsletter, it stated that there   were   movements   afoot   to   implement fragrance-free areas in the workplace. The potential options that a business would have would be these: 1) divide the workplace up into areas designated for smokers, areas designated for non-smokers, and areas designated for those who wished to avoid any fragrances; 2) divide the workplace into non-smoking areas and fragrance-free areas; or 3) eliminate all smoking and all fragrances from the entire premises.

What are we really addressing here? Is it just a matter of health or the preference of air not polluted by perfumed fragrances? Or are we addressing something far more important, and that is your rights and my rights in relationship to the greater picture? Is anything really being addressed or are we just being swayed by a group of fanatical, egotistical, self-serving bullies?

The question is: How can some people be so up-in-arms against breathing in cigarette smoke and some people be so up-in-arms against breathing in fragrances, and yet seem to be completely oblivious to the extremely dangerous and deadly toxins that are emitted by the tons daily through the tailpipes of their cars? What of the men and the women who use aerosol cans filled with hairspray and underarm deodorant propelled by extremely dangerous fluoro-carbons that have been proven to destroy the ozone layer? The continued use of fluorocarbons will, in a very few years, destroy the ozone layer to the point where we will no longer be able to leave our homes unless we are totally shielded from the rays of the sun. The consequences of not using such protection will certainly guarantee skin cancers of all kinds.

I wonder if these people who are so worried about second-hand smoke and perfumed fragrances are as worried about the preservatives and nitrates that abound in our food supply, ultimately weakening our physical body. Do these same individuals become outraged at the extended shelf-life expectancy of the foods that they purchase at their supermarkets? Are these people as outraged about aspartame, which is so potentially dangerous? Are these same people as outraged by the rampant use and availability of drugs in our society? Are these people as outraged by the permissiveness of our society that has brought about the world-wide plague of AIDS? Are these people as outraged by the vast numbers of poor and homeless in such a wealthy society? Are these people as outraged by the selfish attitude of our society that states, I want what I want no matter what it may cost you? But then fanaticism has never been controlled by good common sense and logic.

We should all take a more discerning look at our society, at our world, and not be so hypocritical. Maybe we should join together and demand a drug-free society. Maybe we should join together and demand a society that provides shelter for the homeless. Maybe we should demand a society that has enough self-respect to be outraged against the permissiveness toward open sex that has led to a plague so immense that by the year 2000 we will have six to eight million individuals dying of AIDS in this country.

I just wonder if there are not more important things than a smoke-free area or a fragrance-free area. I just wonder when the American public will stop allowing itself to be distracted from the really important factors concerning our health and our happiness and our spirituality. Maybe it is time we as individuals stop being so gullible, allowing others to slip a ring through our nose and lead us around to do their bidding.

May the Peace and Joy
Of the Infinite Father
Always be with you,
And may the Joy of His Son
Always be present with you
And may His Light shine down
Upon you all
And around you
And within you.

Self-centeredness breeds loneliness.
It is the willful murder of joy
that rightfully belongs to the soul.

Chapter 11

Activists for a Higher Cause

I have been fortunate to have always had an animal in my life. I remember as a very small child that my two brothers had a number of large white rabbits. I also remember my grandmother had a pet chicken that was as tame as any dog could be.

For years, I begged my mother and father to let me have my own dog. At the age of seven or eight, my parents finally gave in to my constant pleas. I was permitted to have the dog, providing I would assume full responsibility for that dog and see to the dog's needs of food, water, and exercise. Our family did not believe that pets should be chained up or locked in small cages. My brothers' rabbits had the freedom of the small backyard. Even the chickens roamed free. The dog that I received was taught to take its proper place in the family and in the home. Since my parents did not believe in chaining a dog up, the dog was taught that certain rooms in the home were off limits. It was my responsibility to teach the dog that it was not permitted on the furniture. Also, after I left the dog out to do its business, it was my business to clean up after the dog and place the natural fertilizer in the compost pile at the end of the yard.

Since that first dog, I have been privileged to have four wonderful companions. My wife and I were very lucky because all of our dogs lived many years and died of old age, with the exception of the first dog that we acquired after moving to our farm. For some unknown reason, Spike decided to venture up to the main road at the end of our lane and was hit by a car. It was much like losing a close member of our family. In all the years that we had Spike, he had never walked the quarter of a mile up the lane to the main road. Why he chose to do so that day still remains a mystery to us.

I am very thankful that the woman that hit Spike was kind enough to come to our home and inform us. I promptly took Spike to a veterinarian. Unfortunately, Spike was unable to overcome the damage done to him. After an appropriate length of time, we acquired another dog.

Living in farm country was very satisfying. We became very attached to the horses and cows from neighboring farms that grazed on our land. We were amazed to discover that horses and cows have unique personalities, just as dogs do.

As a child I was taught that animals must be treated with the same respect and compassion that you treat a member of your family. I was also taught that animals have a place in life and a purpose in life just as you and I have. I know from personal experience that the dogs that we had were not mindless unfeeling animals. I realized very early in life that my pets had a natural sensitivity that proved they were not stupid, unfeeling creatures. I can recall many episodes, as a child and as an adult, where it was very apparent by the dogs' actions that they were feeling the same feelings that we were. I learned that I was not a master over these dogs but I was a caretaker and a companion to them.

I recall very clearly one particular episode when my wife, Nancy, had become very sick. Our dog, Prince, lay beside her bed as though he were guarding her from the rest of the world. This was not Prince's normal behavior. He was a very frisky and playful German shepherd. But during the time of Nancy's sickness, he was very quiet and very protective of her. I can recall many times when I had a migraine headache, Prince would lay at the foot of the bed very quietly. When Prince would decide to leave the foot of my bed, he would leave so quietly you would swear he tiptoed out of the room.

Our dogs were not just pets. They were members of our family, members that we loved dearly. I have always been against cruelty to animals. It is my belief that an individual who will deliberately mistreat an animal will also mistreat a fellow human being.

A few years ago there was a movement to stop the slaughter of baby seals. These helpless little animals were clubbed across the head and then skinned for their fur. Many of these baby seals were not dead before the hunters began to skin them. I saw some photographs of these helpless little animals being slaughtered. It went against every fiber in my body. How inhumane can an individual be to kill a baby seal just because its fur is as white as the snow? It has been my experience in life that man can be very inhuman when it comes to the all-mighty dollar.

I could accept the need to kill an animal for its fur, providing the hunter used that fur to keep himself or his family warm, particularly if it would be a true hardship for them to purchase ready-made coats that would protect them from the Arctic freezes. Were these baby seals being killed to provide a warm fur coat for the hunter or for a member of his family? No. These seals were being killed so that their fur could be used for a coat that was not meant to keep an individual warm but to satisfy the indulgent ego of someone.

More recently, hundreds of people put forth a marvelous effort to save three whales that were trapped by ice. It was a beautiful demonstration of man's compassion and concern when hundreds of people literally hand cut a channel to the open sea so that the whales would not die.

Organizations that protect endangered species are important, and groups that inform us of our responsibility for the proper treatment of animals have their place. But we must keep in mind that in protecting the animals' rights we do not infringe upon human rights. Some animal activist groups have gone so far as to physically and verbally accost people wearing fur coats. This carries the issue too far. We have the responsibility to inform people. But we do not have the right to physically abuse them in order to change their arrogant ignorance or self-indulgence. We should have a significant voice in the protection of our animals today so that our children and their children will be able to experience the pleasures and joys that those animals can give. Those minority groups who attempt to physically force their beliefs on the majority of the people should not be condoned.

A number of questions deeply plague my soul. Are these animal activists, who are so enraged at the killing of animals, also as enraged at the killing of unborn babies? How can we eliminate the senseless killing of animals if we do not have the moral conscience to cease the killing of unborn babies? How can we be so incensed at the trapping of rabbits and the shooting of deer and be so silent when millions of unborn babies have been murdered in the name of convenience? How can man ascend to such a high degree of compassion to hand chop a canal through the ice to save three whales and then stoop to such depths of depravity to abort an unborn child?

This is a serious situation that those who are sincerely interested in spiritual concepts must address sooner or later. We in the spiritual movement should be fully aware that a soul of an individual can be present in that fetus at the moment of conception. By killing the fetus, we are depriving that soul of an opportunity to grow. This is the only way as spiritual metaphysicians we can look at the abortion of a child. We are not God. Therefore, we do not know for a fact what the future might have been or was to be for that incoming soul. We as true spiritual seekers must realize the horrendous ramifications in respect to karma that abortion presents to the individuals involved and to the society that allows it. How conveniently hypocrisy can blind an individual!

Man's rules are not pliable
And are not bending;
They are rigid,
So consequently, they can be broken,
Or they can be changed.
God's rules are made in love,
Consequently, they are firm;
They are strong;
They are good;
They are fair;
They are rigid;
But they become elastic and bendable
With love as the tempering element.
God's Laws will not be broken,
But they will bend to meet you
As you stretch to reach them.
This is the Love of your Father.

*Looking only for the best in others
we wisely see the flaws in ourselves.*

Chapter 12

Reflections on Forgiveness

If you do something horrible to me and I forgive you for that action, can I assume therefore that you do not have a karmic debt involved from that particular action toward me?

The straight answer to this question is: Your forgiveness of that individual does not eliminate that person's karma brought on by his actions toward you.

We must remember that we are all individually responsible for our own karma that we create. In the situation described in this question, if the individual would have returned the horrible deed with another horrible deed or hatred to the person, then the individual would have created karma for himself. In addition to that, that individual would have tied himself karmically to the person who originally perpetrated the horrible deed. This lack of forgiveness could have entangled those two people into an inescapable maze of karmic debt.

Individuals who prefer to forgive as opposed to hating practice forgiveness from the heart; in actuality elevate themselves that much closer to their godly state. You cannot eliminate the karmic debt of someone else. The very best that can be done is to forgive those individuals and bless them with a positive thought or prayer. If we do not forgive others their misdeeds against us, we have in essence allowed them to drag us down to their level. By forgiving others who trespass against us, we activate the Christ Consciousness within us and in so doing we move that much closer to The God and demonstrate the god that is within each one of us.

Consider the effects on those who are lacking in forgiveness, who are resentful and full of hate. The medical community has discovered that, within eight to sixteen months after an emotionally traumatic situation, the individual who has undergone the trauma will undergo a serious ailment that in some cases has even brought on their death. In these situations the strongest emotions involved were resentment, a lack of forgiveness, and hatred. These three emotions existed either individually or in different combinations.

Why does this happen? Why is it we suffer when we are not forgiving or are resentful or filled with hate? The answer to this is very simple: All these emotions cannot really be directed toward another individual. They are reflections of self. Whenever we hate others, we are not really hating them, but we are hating the god that is within them. And that god that is within them is the same god that is within us. Therefore in essence what we are doing is hating the god that is within ourselves. This begins a chain reaction within us, a chain reaction of self-punishment or even self-destruction, and in effect we begin to punish the element of our being which is the weakest expression of our total selves, the physical body. This punishment shows up as an ailment that will differ in the degree of severity.

The other element that we must consider, is that if the lack of forgiveness, the resentment, the hate are strong enough, we will eventually act upon them. These actions will more or less be directed against the person that is the object of these emotions. This action begins to weave a web of karmic entrapment that may cost us dearly in order to extract ourselves from this self-created prison. Although these emotions may be directed to a specific person, there is no guarantee that that will be the limit or the extent of the effect. If the target individual, for example, is married, certain acts of hate or resentment toward that particular individual may cause him to react in his family situation in a manner that could cause problems for the members of his family, thus making the karmic debt more complicated and involving innocent individuals. This is a very simplistic scenario. In the real life situation, the tentacles of hate, resentment, and lack of forgiveness are generally much more far-reaching and complicated. It would be much wiser to take this energy needed for the negative emotions and direct it to the positive emotion of forgiveness. All the energy used to drag you down is now utilized as a propellant to skyrocket you to a godlier state.

We must begin to think in terms of attuning ourselves to the personal God, to the intimate God. We must remember that God never leaves us. God has never stepped away from us. But all of us, at one time or another, have pushed God away from ourselves. Forgiveness is a major step in returning to that personal relationship with the Divine Source.

Each of you, as we are,
Will evolve eternally.
You are evolving now
With every minute
That comes into your awareness,
It passes, it brings and takes,
It brings and takes, every second,
Every minute, every hour,
Every day, it brings and takes.
You are on a journey of growth.
So use your God-given mind, think.
Be wise enough to realize
That what you cannot accept today,
You may very well accept tomorrow.

Let the heart guide you
on the long journey
to inner peace.

Chapter 13

Two Paths To Travel

In the world of spiritual seekers, there are two basic positions from which we seek spiritual guidance.

The first seeker is the individual who expresses the opinion that spiritual truth and guidance can be acquired from sources of information or non-physical entities that make grandiose pronouncements of their undying love for us. These sources of information most generally flatter us with how wonderful we are and how much they love us and how their only desire is to help us. They also indoctrinate us with the concept that regardless of what they are, our individual choices are perfectly okay, because it is part of our spiritual growth or our spiritual journey.

In the biggest percentage of cases concerning this type of seeker, you will notice that they are not able to commit themselves to much of anything other than what they are particularly interested in at the moment. Usually these periods of interest are short-lived, although at times they can last for long periods. But usually during these long periods when they are interested in a particular source, they are also scouring the landscape of knowledge for sources that allow them a greater freedom. These individuals are the type who only want to hear the beautiful things of how wonderful they are. They are, in essence, not hunting for the truth, but are only seeking verification of their own self-indulgent concepts. These are the individuals who do not believe in judging others. Yet they are the first to set themselves up as holding the absolute truth. They consider those individuals and organizations that do not follow the same line as their own beliefs to be less spiritually evolved or dealing with a lower or a negative source of guidance.

The overall picture of this type of individual is that they are not committed to anything but the exercise of their own will and personal desires. In actuality, they do not recognize that divine principles or divine truths spell out limits as to what is acceptable and what is not acceptable in the presence of the Divine Spirit. These individuals have not grown into the awareness that, by the very fact that we must interact with others, we must have limits within which we are allowed to do what we choose to do.

A simple example: If we choose to raise a family, we must accept the responsibility that naturally occurs in such a situation. It becomes our responsibility to guide those children in a respect for themselves and a respect for divine principle. We do not have the right to have a child and then leave the responsibility of that child's proper education to the whims of chance. If we are truly seeking divine principle or divine truth, we soon begin to realize that these truths or principles point out the limits and boundaries of proper conduct, not only in regard to others but in regard to our own personal self. Those seekers who choose to hear only the cotton-candied words expounded by some sources are only seeking validation of their own personal concept which generally is, if boiled down to its essence, I can do anything I please and not have to bear the responsibility of my thoughts, words, or deeds.

The second type of seeker is what I call the nuts and bolts seeker. These are the true seekers of spirituality, of divine truth and principle. From previous lifetimes they have learned that spiritual growth is a narrow path. They have realized that spiritual growth starts with accepting responsibility for your actions, for your words. These individuals realize very quickly that self-discipline is the means through which they gain control over themselves and over their own lives and destiny. These individuals grow in self-esteem which gives them greater inner strength and greater conviction. These individuals are the type who learn early in their journey that spiritual truths and divine principles dictate strict guidelines by which they must live. They also have learned that it becomes our responsibility to teach others, and in the process of teaching point out the errors in lifestyle that we must avoid. These types of individuals do not always speak of honey and cream. They speak more often of what is proper and what is improper, and they choose to live a life that is proper, responsible, and in accord with divine principle and spiritual truth.

When it comes to spiritual instruction, if we are given a constant diet of how wonderful we are (honey and cream) we will eventually become spiritually sick. True spiritual instructions will tell us what we can do and what we cannot do. Too many people in the New Age movement feel that traditional religious concepts are of no value and in some cases feel that they are falsehoods. A wise man will realize that there is a divine basis to many of the rules and regulations of traditional religions. If we look back at just our recorded history, we will soon realize that certain divine principles and spiritual laws are at the basis of all major religions. Many of the individuals in the New Age movement wish to rid themselves of anything that may hint of what they think is traditional religion. With such arrogance they are in essence throwing out the baby with the bath water. The nuts and bolts seeker realizes that at the basic heart of all traditional religions, past or present, lies the essence of divine principle and spiritual truth. Of the two types of seekers, which will make the real growth in this lifetime? It is the nuts and bolts seeker, for this seeker wants to get the job done. These individuals do not want the fluff. They do not want the words that inflate the ego. They want to know how it really is so they can get down to business, not tomorrow, not today, but NOW. If we try to determine which type of seeker we are and we can identify with one or the other, we are one step ahead because immediately we know if we are on the right path or not. We know if we are on a productive path or a path of self-delusion. If we are somewhere in between, we must make every effort humanly possible to determine very truthfully in which direction we are leaning. Make the decision as to which direction you choose to go and begin your journey. My advice would be to choose the path of the nuts and bolts seeker. They accomplish far more with less effort in a shorter period of time and with far fewer trials and tribulations.

When we get with God completely,
When we are sitting right beside Him
And He has his arms around us
And He tells us how He was born,
If He was born,
Then we will be happy to tell you.
But by that time,
You are going to be here with us too,
So maybe God will allow us
To whisper that little thing
In your ear,
Maybe.

(from the Childrens' Trance)

It is too late to read the handwriting
on the wall if your back is up against it.

Chapter 14

The Male of
Tomorrow

In times gone by, it was the male who sharpened the point of a wooden stick and used it as a crude spear in order to bring down an animal for food. At other times, it was the male who fashioned a stick into a point, thrust it into the soil, and removed it, leaving a hole into which he dropped a few seeds that would be harvested at a later time.

As we look back across history, we see many times when man's role in society was very simple. He was the hunter; he was the warrior; he was the provider. Today, the male's role is not so easily defined. He no longer must go out and hunt and plant to provide food for his family. He no longer must go out and search for high ground on which to build a shelter that would be easily protected from any marauding enemies.

What is the confusion that the male faces in our society today? The overall attitude in American society and in the world as a whole is that the male is still the provider, he is still the hunter, the warrior, the gatherer. Yet, today society also expects him to be sensitive, caring, and loving.

For centuries upon centuries, the male has been placed in a cast-iron mold of hunter, warrior, and provider. In a period of twenty to thirty years, our society has begun to place demands on the male that are totally contradictory to the role that he has been expected to fill. For the majority of males, this contradiction places them in a state of complete confusion. They are expected to be strong and to provide. They are expected to always win and bring home the trophy. Yet at the same time, the male is expected to be sensitive, to be caring, to allow his emotions to be expressed. Suddenly, it is perfectly all right for a man to cry in public.

What the females of our society have not realized about the male's nature is that man is a creature of habit, far more so than the female. The male likes everything reduced to a simple nut-and-bolt technique. The male approaches each experience in life from a position he views as logical. The male is not accustomed to allowing his emotions or his heart to rule. This is not to say that the male is not capable or is not willing. For the male to make such a transition from the warrior and provider to the sensitive husband and father is a tremendous step. Because of his history, the male has no guidelines on how this can be achieved. He has had no real experience in the art of sensitivity as a collective group in society. Because of the mold in which society has placed the male, he is not accustomed to failure nor can he cope with failure as readily as the female can. Therefore, he moves ahead very cautiously.

The potential for the male to become sensitive and loving is there. As we all know, at a spiritual level, we are both male and female, we are androgynous. We assume one nature, either male or female, according to the lesson or lessons to be learned in a particular lifetime. If man is ever, as a collective group, to become sensitive, i.e. his actions and attitudes moderated by love and compassion, it is necessary for the female to guide the male in that direction, encouraging him when he attempts to display a gentle side of his nature.

As the male is released from his bondage as the hunter, warrior, and provider, he begins to set himself up as an example to the male children in his family. They in turn will begin to learn from the example of the father that part of the male nature is to be sensitive, is to show love, and is to be compassionate. In this situation the children will have a personal model or example to follow.

If the female chooses to release the male from his bondage, she must create the environment in which the male may begin to step away from society's mold. The impetus for change for most men lies in their partner, their mate. The male receives signals and translates those signals into actions and attitudes. If the male is ever to be able to reach the state of sensitivity he should and can achieve, it can only come through the proper environment created by his mate.

Just as the female creates the spirituality of tomorrow by the spiritual instructions she gives her children today, so will she create the state of the male and his attitudes and outlooks toward life that he will have tomorrow.

The male holds within his make-up the sensitive and loving male. The female holds within her make-up the avenue through which the male can be re-created and released from his historical bondage. In man's history, there have been a number of men who have achieved sensitivity and compassion. Behind these men were the mates that made the pathway available to their fulfillment. At the heart and soul of the male is sensitivity, compassion, and love, but the door must be unlocked for them so that they may venture forth.

As with all things, the expressed sensitivity of the male lies in the hands of the reality-makers of tomorrow, the female, the instrument of manifestation.

A godly state is a state of activity,
Constant progression;
Negativity is totally opposite,
It is the stagnant condition;
It is the static condition.
In itself it has no motion;
It weighs heavily.
For it to move as the Divine moves,
It must be carried.
Hear then:
Those who subscribe to negativity
Carry a burden;
Those who subscribe to the will
Of the Divine
Are carried.

Helping children build character
will develop our own.

Chapter 15

The Good Parents

In our society today, parent bashing is the "in" thing. Psychologists are giving us all kinds of excuses for our own laziness. "Well, I was abused as a child." There isn't a person on the face of the earth that can't say they were abused as a child. But what constitutes abuse? Parents aren't always the smartest of people. They will probably raise their children as they have been raised. But previous generations didn't have quite the same problems we have today. When they were children no one set them on a pedestal and said: "Oh, what a wonderful thing you are, you're God's gift to me. You're so smart, you can do anything."

But once a child steps out of the door of his home he is stepping into an alien world. That world outside the door of the home will do more damage to a child than any damage that can be done in the family situation. Sure, there are some situations where parents really do abuse their children in the worst sort of ways. But those are few and far between. Recently a woman said to me, "I'm afraid to even holler at my kid for fear that she is going to tell her teacher that she was abused and then the social workers are going to come around causing problems." And that has happened. It's a sad situation when parents become frightened of their children. We have been and still are far too liberal with our children and we're paying the consequences for it.

There comes a time when a child must learn that the only security, the only safety zone in their life is in their home. No matter how bad it's been they'll never be treated as badly in the home as they could be outside of the home. Someone said: "You know, Bill, I can give you example after example where children have been really seriously abused." I said: "I'm sure. But is the child living and breathing?" "Yes, yes." What about the kid that went outside the home and was shot to death? I certainly am not for beating children, but whether we look at the Bible or any of the other spiritual writings in man's history, present and past, there's one constant truism —spare the rod and spoil the child. When we find this concept in all spiritual writings we have to stop and think, "Now wait, is this one of the Divine Principles?"

If we listen to the "experts" on child rearing, we end up with the moral condition that we have right now. Yet we'll find very few experts agree with one another. They originally came out with the idea, "Don't intimidate your child, don't hit your child. Let your child express itself." We have to use a little common sense when it comes to growth. We have to have guidelines for development in any area, whether it's learning how to socialize or learning how to do your job or learning how to become more spiritual. We have to have some fundamental guidelines to move along to show us the direction. When it comes to children, if we do nothing to traumatize them, how are they ever going to deal with life? How many people find that when they deal with people outside of their family, in their jobs, in their shopping, they never run across others that have done them in? You've never been done in, never had a problem, you've been treated absolutely wonderfully, courteously, it's been just a picnic away from your home situation. When you spent ten dollars for something, you got twelve back in value. No. You see, you walk out into the real world, it's a cold, cruel place.

How are children going to learn to deal with such a cold and cruel society if they don't experience some of it within the family unit? Certainly, a mother and a father will be stern and in some cases in the eyes of the child, cruel, because they exercise discipline. In a normal situation that parent is not going to beat the child nearly as badly as if that child had been punished by a total stranger and the total stranger had no emotional ties with that individual child. This idea of never upsetting little Sally or little Jimmy with a paddling or a reprimand is pure stupidity. You can't be a friend to your children, you have to be a parent, you have to be an example. Why aren't we? Why do we need experts telling us: "Well, if you can't deal with life it's because you were abused and you have a wounded child within you and you have to go through this healing process." Why do we have to have people like that? Because we don't love ourselves enough to have enough respect for ourselves to pick ourselves up and make the best of the situation.

The experts play on a very common weakness that we all have, allowing us to wallow in our own self-pity. They say, "Oh, it's okay that your life is a mess and you don't do anything with it. You can't because your mom and dad made you eat those green beans when you didn't want to. That really did you terrible damage." Kids can bounce back from so many things it's unbelievable. A parent does more damage to that child when the parent says over and over again, "Please, Jimmy don't touch that," talking to this little kid as if he were a grown adult who could comprehend what he was doing. The child doesn't know what it's doing. He doesn't know what he is doing because he hasn't been taught the right or wrong of what he is doing. A child doesn't have a built-in sense of right and wrong or proper conduct. It is the duty of the parents to teach them proper conduct in each situation. Certainly going to a store and handling all the merchandise and knocking it on the floor and breaking jars is not proper conduct for an adult or a child. But how much is that child going to learn when the mother continually says every time she goes to the grocery store: "Please don't do that. Mommy said 'No.'" The child isn't going to learn anything. The child's going to say: "That piece of putty is gonna tell me what to do? She just likes to hear herself talk." Kids are not smart but they are not stupid. They are clever. That parent isn't the master of that child, the child is the master of the parent. A parent is like that, whether it's the mother or the father, simply because at a soul level that parent doesn't like itself. That parent doesn't love and respect itself. And it shows in the fact that it's not going to take control of the situation and do the job properly. Whatever the reason the soul doesn't like itself is really immaterial. What is important is that you like yourself. There's no reason why you shouldn't, and if you do it benefits more than just you, it helps your children.

The child must learn in the family structure that there are limits and modes of conduct that it must adhere to if it is to survive in the world outside of the home. The parents may paddle their child but the world could just as easily kill that same child for committing the same act outside of the home.

May the Peace and Joy
That we have in our state of existence
One day be yours;
And may the Love
That we experience from our Creator,
From our God,
Be equally shared with each
And every one of you.

Mankind wants to acknowledge Negativity,
but not as something negative.

Chapter 16

The Light Versus The Darkness

Any literature dealing with spirituality, any literature that is a part of a major religious or spiritual belief system that has been around for a while, talks about an evilness or a negativity or a demonic figure. Such literature also says that we are spirit beings. How are we to relate this physical body with a spiritual body, in this sense: If I do something immoral, God's going to put me in Hell to burn for an eternity? What is there to burn, if I'm a spirit being? I know for a fact that when I die my body gets thrown in a hole some place, rots and becomes nothing, but that isn't me. So how can a soul be put in Hell and burn? There has to be something to burn. First of all, fire is of the earth. So what is the

Church, what is religion, what are spiritual writings trying to tell us? Well, first of all, they do indeed tell us there is a negative force. It not only has to do with actual negative beings but it also has to do with an attitude.

Whatever name we wish to use for immorality or negativity, we're still talking about the same entity and the same attitude. If we check the evolvement of whatever these words are, Satan, Lucifer, the Devil, we find they all go back to a description of an action. This is important: It's a description of an action. What does the Devil, what does Satan mean to us? It means the Accuser, the Deceiver. And what are these terms trying to say to us? They are trying to say that the name is not as important as what the concept conveys to us. First of all, we are spirit beings or conscious state beings and we are only using these physical bodies so that we can grow closer to our God. This is the mode that we work in right now. But when we die we revert to our original form which is a spirit being. That means we don't have a body, at least not in the sense that we understand a body. It's not flesh and bones. It is a conscious state. We really can't fathom what that means so we say a glorified body or a soul. There's nothing to burn in a soul because it is spirit. There's nothing tangible. So when religions or spiritual concepts say we're going to go to Hell and burn, what is there to burn?

Well, before we can answer what burns and what kind of punishment is there, we have to understand where the concept of Hell came from. Hell is what we call it. But when we go back to the original concept found in the Bible it was the word "Sheol" which means the netherland or the shadowland or the underworld. That means that it's an area that is not related to the light. The Shadowland or the Land of the Shadows is the most common concept used.

Some will say "But I know there's a Hell because Christ said you burn in the fires of Gehenna." But, what is Gehenna? Hell? No. That's what we say it is but that isn't what it truly is. Gehenna was a dump outside Jerusalem. That's where they threw the garbage, they threw dead animals and every once in a while a dead body. It was a great valley or pit that was constantly burning. It had black smoke rising out of it all of the time. It burned twenty-four hours a day. Christ said that Sheol is like that; the darkness of the smoke, the consuming of what was not good and useful. This is the netherland where the discards went. So, Hell has nothing to do with fire. That's a very literal or fundamentalistic translation, which is not an accurate translation. Christ was talking about a place where discards were dumped and it was dark because over Gehenna the smoke was so black that the sunlight didn't filter into the pit. So, this is where we get the concept of fires of Hell, where we get the concept of people burning forever. But what Christ was saying is that Sheol is dark like the clouds cutting off the sunlight, and that all the discards went there, the garbage, because they had not been useful. How do we understand it then in terms of what happens to us? We don't have a physical body after we die, we are a spiritual body. And if we are spiritual only there is nothing to burn.

The relationship to burning and a spiritual body is the zeal. Zeal as it was used in those days is a spiritual fire inside that causes us to be strongly motivated. It's a driving force inside of us. The fire, the burning, is going to be the zealous desire that we have to walk within the Light and realize that we didn't make it into God's heavenly realm. The dross, the negativity, is "burned off" by the "fire," the zeal.

The Devil doesn't want our souls. What's he going to do with them? Does he have a palace there where he stockpiles them? No. He doesn't want our souls. He doesn't have any use for them. The purpose of the Devil or Lucifer is to accuse us of our lack of godliness. You see, if he can get us to think we're not godly, he has succeeded. He doesn't want the Divine Light to show. At one time he was the beacon of the Divine Light. But now his ultimate goal is to diminish or extinguish this Divine Light. If he can get us to forget about our godliness, he has completed his task. He doesn't want the Divine Truth to spread.

The Devil exists in a state of darkness. Darkness is a turning away from the Light and a looking into our own shadow. As a conscious state being, you are very transparent to light coming to you. As it comes to you, you enhance that light and spread it out. As you are facing the light, the light is coming in and going out, radiating out from you. But if you turn your back to the light, you have nothing but shadow or darkness in front of you. So Hell is one's looking into one's own shadow. You see, you have no longer allowed the Light to lead you. You have decided you are the light in yourself and you walk your own path.

The nature of God is to be extremely loving, to be extremely giving. An all-loving and an all-giving father would not chastise his child unjustly. He would not permanently kick his child out of his presence without ever giving that child the opportunity to return. If he were to do that, that child would have had to commit some grievous offense, not against the father but against himself. The position of a father is to teach a child not to offend himself. And in order not to offend yourself, you have to live within a certain structure or framework. Well, that framework is the Divine Truth, the Divine State. When we go against that, we're not hurting God. How could we possibly hurt Him? We are a mere spark of that Divine Essence. What is important is what we're doing to ourselves. In harming ourselves we always hurt others as well.

God does not judge us. There is no tally sheet when we die that sends us to Heaven, or condemns us to Hell. An all-loving God cannot also be a condemning God. It's a contradiction. The sum total of your life will be reviewed by you yourself. Because we are made in the likeness and image of God, because we have that seed of God within us, we are capable of judging ourselves according to Divine Principles. We have a Divine Truth inside that says when we cross over, when we go through the process of death, when we go to review our previous, our past life, the one we just lived, we're going to say: "OK, what did I do the ten seconds after I was born; what did I do thirty seconds after I was born; what did I do twenty-one years, thirteen days and fourteen hours and seventeen seconds after I was born; what did I do fifty-five years, six months, two weeks, three hours and thirty-one seconds?" We will review our entire life, second by second by second and the scale of judgment will be the Christ-consciousness that's in us. Satan is the deceiver that allows us to wallow in our own darkness, and to rationalize our existence instead of living the Christ Consciousness that exists within us.

In the eyes of God,
This Divine and Glorious Creator,
Only the good is seen,
And so as each of you
Molding and working towards
Your rightful position,
You too must practice that inner sight
Of seeing only the good.
Pass no judgment on others,
Because with the judgment
That you pass on them,
You have condemned yourself.
If you can look at each individual you know,
At each individual you meet,
And see one spark of goodness
In that individual,
You have one foot in the door
Of the God-made heavenly realms.

Life has brought us many opportunities
to love and be loved,
and many have we squandered.

Chapter 17

The Essence of a Spiritual Person

What is the essence of a spiritual life? What is the essence of a spiritual person? What is the difference between a spiritual person and a person that is not considered spiritual? The basic difference is the attitude in which they approach each day of their life. Spirituality is determined by the attitudes that we have and the way we act upon those attitudes. A person who is not spiritual is dealing with a negative attitude. An attitude is not what we say with our mouths, it is what we do with our own personal lives and the lives that we affect, influence, or come in contact with. In other words, what do we think of ourselves and how do we treat ourselves? How do we think of others and how do we treat others?

The basic building block of a negative person is selfishness infused with laziness. Selfishness in the sense that these people choose to serve themselves first before they consider anything or anyone else. They feel that they have a right to have all their wishes and desires filled without the effort of work. In other words, if they desire something it should be theirs. They shouldn't have to work for it. They shouldn't have to put any effort forth other than just the wanting of it. If, in some rare instances, they do make an effort to earn what they want instead of taking, the effort put forth, at very best, is a very minimal attempt that is of a very short duration. It is basically nothing more than a display of showmanship or bravado that they can use to fool themselves and others into believing that they have done all that they could do. Their lamenting cries echo through the empty halls of self-pity, "Well, I tried. I did everything possible."

The revealing trait of this type of person is that they always have an excuse for their actions. They are cowards when it comes to commitment and responsibility. In this cowardliness they run from the very commitments and responsibilities that could make them strong and brave. These individuals do not seek self-esteem through work and commitment. This attitude goes for materialistic possessions and most assuredly for relationships. These individuals, because of their self-serving ego and their laziness, cannot find an identity in themselves. Their identity comes from what items or things that they possess. Their identity comes from the individuals that they control and manipulate to satisfy whatever desires they may have.

On a list of priorities the very last thing these individuals consider is the other individuals around them. They place themselves so far above others that they are incapable of seeing anyone else, let alone the needs of others. They are individuals that cannot make a commitment and fulfill that commitment, regardless of the time. They may be able to fool themselves into making a commitment and feeling as though they have fulfilled that commitment, but their commitment only lasts as long as whatever they have committed to has served them and their personal needs. Their commitments are much like the winds that blow across a sterile desert. They move the lifeless grains of sand from mound to mound, changing the terrain moment to moment, with the same empty lifelessness as a universe seared by the fires of deceit. For, in fact, these individuals have practiced the greatest deceit and that is they have deceived themselves. They have thrown away the opportunity to bear fruit and bring it to its maturity. These individuals are completely insensitive to the needs, let alone the wants, of others. Their sole purpose for existing is their own personal gratification. These are the individuals who will say to you, "I love you," and with the next breath betray you.

Let us take a look at a person who is truly spiritual. Truly spiritual people also think of themselves. They respect themselves. They know that they have something to offer that only they can offer. The respect that they have for themselves is a healthy respect because they love themselves. They love themselves because their existence is focused on reaching out, not taking in. They have stumbled onto the secret of spirituality: it is not what you take unto yourself but it is what issues forth from you. It is not what you take that makes you happy, but it is what you give that makes you happy.

Thus, a day of happiness for them has been a day of giving and sharing. They are not engulfed in their own sensitivity. They are acutely aware of the need to be sensitive to those around them. The compassion and the sensitivity to the needs of others is reflected back to them through the words and the deeds that they have freely and unconditionally given to others. These individuals do not seek to receive, they seek to alleviate, to build, to create. They seek to assume the responsibility and carry the burden so that others may walk more freely and more erect.

These individuals will have the same fear of commitment and responsibility as a negative person. A fundamental difference is that the spiritual person accepts that fear and rises above it into bravery and honor. A spiritual person does not wear his heart on his sleeve. He keeps his heart in its proper place and shares from that place. A spiritual person lives life moment-by-moment, day-by-day, allowing that beautiful experience of life to bring to him the opportunities to be compassionate, to be loving, and to share the burden of those around him.

This is the essence of our purpose. This is the mystery of life. This is the secret to spirituality. This is the pathway of the enlightened ones. This is the presence of God and Christ within each one of us. Where does it start? With those that we have commitments to: our families, our loved ones, our friends, and our neighbors. A spiritual person opens up and reaches out to give and to fulfill, to bring some measure of happiness, to bring some measure of a smile.

This is an ordinary day in the life of a spiritual person.

How feebly man creates his heaven,
And how gloriously God creates His,
For His and with His.
Choose now while you can
What avenue you will walk;
Choose well and choose wisely.

When life seems to have lost all purpose,
the purpose is to start anew.

Chapter 18

Perfection In An Imperfect World

Something imperfect cannot hold perfection. Material reality, in itself, because it is imperfect, cannot hold perfection. The material world that we understand exists because of our imperfection. We chose to separate ourselves from the perfect state we had with the Divine. But in His Love for us, The Divine Essence sent a vibration out so that even though we chose to be imperfect, we would be set in a reality where we could practice our godliness back to perfection. The Divine Source, knowing that we had free will, provided for us a set of vibrations that we could tap into to create what we needed to realize our godly perfection. To keep from being discouraged, to keep from being spiritually depressed, the activity of the physical manifestation demanded that a lesser amount of higher vibration would have to be used. In other words, the full power that we have, the higher vibrations that we have, cannot really be incorporated into the material manifestation, since the material manifestation is a set of vibrations based on a denser form. It is a denser form because it contains less spiritual energy. It is a neutral set of vibrations, neither positive nor negative. The application of these neutral vibrations determines whether they are positive or negative. Since these vibrations are being used by beings that are less than perfect (us after leaving the Godhead), that set of vibrations will tend toward a gray area, rather than the pure white light of perfection.

Because the light of true perfection does not reflect on that set of vibrations that is the material world, it cannot take the higher vibration of Spirituality. Since we are no longer with the Divine, the higher vibration we have is less pure. Now, if we were to step aside and let the Divine Light shine on the physical world instead of our own light, which is diminished, it could take that perfection. It would take that perfection, absorb it and in that sense, it would become perfect. The minute we apply the Divine to imperfection, it is no longer imperfect, it is no longer material or physical, it is spiritual. Once spirituality of the proper degree is applied to something, it becomes perfect, therefore it is no longer material, it is then spiritual. Once a spiritual vibration of a higher degree is touched to something material, it automatically becomes perfect. It loses the grossness of the physical and becomes spiritual. In our sense, in our reality, it no longer exists but in the true reality it does exist in its perfect form. The higher self, pure vibration, overcomes the shadow of that pure vibration, the shadow cast by ourselves, the shadow that would block out the purest vibration which is Divine.

There must be a way to connect the higher self and the material level that the light is not shining on. The physical container is attempting to deal with a brilliant light only after traveling through a pitch-black maze, a task that is next to impossible. Once in a while a way is found to pierce that black maze, and that encourages us to continue on even though it appears we are in an almost hopeless situation. There are constant "radio signals" or spiritual impulses being put out by the source of this black maze, the source being our higher self, the creator of the maze. The spiritual impulse is the little voice inside that was once called the conscience. It is the impulse or the radio wave that your higher self provides to guide you through the maze you have created. Listen to it and you will move through that maze without problems. Once in a while you might stumble to test your sincerity. Only to test your sincerity, to make sure that what this divine being, your higher self, has created, is created perfectly and not a miscreation or a self-delusion. So every once in a while, even though you follow what is right, you stumble and fall. That is to test your sincerity to see whether what is coming out of your mouth is based on what's in your heart or just what the surrounding conditions would expect you to say. Since every one of us is bound to the same process of development, we found it helpful to say to one another, "Let's work together. Instead of me just traveling through a pitch-black maze, let's turn on some lights, let's create a globe, an earth, some grass, some water, etc. and let's create some physical bodies that we can manipulate as master puppets to go through this maze, this proving ground, helping each other to attain our perfection and eliminating the darkness."

Nobody is here to help me and I am certainly not here to help anybody. I'm here to look out for one person and that's me. I could be a saint that floated in the air and I could do everything, bless you and feed you and tell you all the truths there are in the heavens and it won't do you a bit of good. It can't help you one iota if you don't want to accept it. And my desire to help you has to be based on my desire to help myself. How am I helping myself? Here's where a spiritual greed comes in that's good greed. Now that may sound like a terrible thing because the minute we say greed, it has a negative connotation. This spiritual greed is not negative. It is greed in the sense that it is an all-consuming desire or thirst for spiritual perfection. You have a right and an obligation and a responsibility to correct yourself, to take care of yourself first. If you don't take care of yourself first you can't take care of anyone else. The only way in this maze that we have

created, the only way that we can take care of ourself first is by working with each other. So if I'm a
very compassionate person—well, I may think that
I'm really compassionate when in fact the higher self
says: "I am compassionate because I'm looking out
for myself." But if it makes our cooperation with
others a little easier then fine, we can think that
we're helping each other because we love each
other. We're all helping ourselves because we love
ourselves. Spiritual greed is good but we must understand it is not the kind of greed that we normally
understand as greed. It's a driving hunger, a respect
and self-esteem for yourself that is all-encompassing.
It is a fire inside, driving you to do anything to
maintain that godly self-esteem, that godly self-
respect, that godly self-love.

In the earthly reality, as we understand it, we
are all solid. We are all working at our jobs, at our
lives; it's all very real to us as individuals. We're
working with a common reality, a common denominator, so everybody has an equal right to achieve
their highest potential according to the efforts that
they put forth. But how real is all this? It isn't real at
all. It is an illusion. It doesn't really exist. You may
be thinking: "I'm me, I know I'm me, I can feel myself. When I look in the mirror, I see my face, I see
the color of my eyes, my hair, I see the clothes I'm
wearing." No, I'm afraid that is not you. That is not
real. It is 100% illusion. But it is a whole creation, a
whole universe that we have created. We have all
agreed, even though we have created our own

world, our own universe, to create from the same common denominator so that everybody can progress through life with an equal opportunity to grow spiritually. A simple example: What I see as an apple, you see as an apple. What you see as an orange, I see as an orange. What is a Divine Principle, you should recognize as a Divine Principle and so should I. You don't have an advantage over me and I don't have an advantage over you. It is a godly fairness that gives us all the same chance to reach our perfection.

The highest essence of ourself still has the spark of God. The spark of God, the essence of life, and the Christ Consciousness are the same thing. The names change according to the activity. What's the difference between the Holy Spirit, Christ, and God; God the Father, God the Son, and the Holy Spirit? God the Father is the source of Divine Principle, God the Son or the Christ Consciousness is the knowledge of Divine Principle, and the Holy Spirit is the action of bringing those Divine Principles into the reality of our daily lives by actually living those Divine Principles. The three aspects of God are the same Force acting in different ways. It's the same with ourselves, when we talk about ourselves—the Christ Consciousness, the spark of God, the breath of God, whatever the terminology. That is the highest purest essence of yourself that has been touched directly by God. That's God's finger on you, and it is through that touching that the purity or the perfection of you exists. It's in you. But that purity cannot exist in the part of you that is not perfect. That part of you that is not perfect exists because of the conscious you which made choices against the higher self's knowledge. In other words, the higher self cannot truly exist in full manifestation in material form because the higher self is perfect, it's the finger of God within us. The higher self cannot exist in the physical because of the physical's imperfection, but this imperfection can exist within the perfect of the higher self. The imperfect only exists as an avenue to manifesting perfection. Now that is the key. It is only an avenue of manifesting perfection because we have chosen it to exist. It is a creation of our own making, therefore we must uncreate it through the process of manifesting Divine Principle in our life. In essence, what we have created as imperfect becomes our avenue back to total perfection.

We have learned
To tell you the truth,
With complete love
And complete understanding.
We have learned
To be able to tell you
Of those things
That you have done wrong,
And not condemn you,
But understand completely
And still love you.
We have learned
That when you ask us for advice,
And we give it to you,
And you do not follow it,
We have learned
That we still love you,
And we still pray for you.

*Only in eternity will the
soul find tranquillity.*

Chapter 19

Putting Prayer To Work

We believe that prayer consists of saying to God, "Please make this happen, or please let this happen." That may be the general understanding of prayer, but that isn't what prayer is at all. When we pray for something, it is natural to ask something of God, but in praying for something we must assume a certain responsibility in working with that prayer. "Working" with a prayer means conducting ourselves in a way consistent with the goal of the prayer. Our prayer loses meaning if our actions are immoral, if our attitude does not support what our lips say. So when we see a world praying for something and the prayer does not appear to be answered, it's because the world is giving the situation lip service.

As an example let's assume there is a war and the people on both sides of that war are praying to God. Since we are a part of the Western belief system, let's also assume they are Christians. By dealing with the Christian aspects we may gain a clearer picture. Two Christian countries go to war, and in the one country, all the mothers and fathers are praying that they win the war and their sons come home alive. In the other country, all the parents, brothers, and sisters are also praying that they win the war and their loved ones come home alive. Only one country wins the war. Is it because God has favorites, and has answered the prayers of only one side? Was it God's thought, "Well, I like these people over here a little better than I like those." No. When we pray, the verbalizing of the prayer is the final step in an attitude that must be developed. If the verbalization comes before the attitude, it takes that much longer for the prayer to work, if it's going to work at all. The reason why most prayers don't seem to be answered is this: We want the answer to our prayers placed on a silver platter and served to us. This attitude smacks of wanting something for nothing or, at very best, an hour's labor for eight hours' pay. We have to assume the responsibility of working with that prayer and the situation so the prayer can manifest itself. In essence, it takes a mental attitude and the physical activities that support that mental attitude.

Many metaphysical groups consider prayer merely to be a positive force, a vibration that one sends out. It is, but it's only a positive force and a vibration that you're sending out if you are in accord with the prayer. If you're not in accord with the prayer, then you are sending out conflicting messages, conflicting signals. The words you say are one form of power or vibration. The mental activity, the visualization inherent in the prayer is another form of vibration or power that you're sending out. If the voice or the word is saying one thing and the heart or the visualization, the internal you, is saying something else, you're canceling out your prayer. Or even worse, you're sending out mixed signals that are causing confusion, distraction, dissension. When a prayer is answered, it's because all the elements were in place and all were working together.

We have to be willing to work within a situation to make the prayer come alive or to manifest. An example: A person has family problems and prays for guidance; they pray to resolve the problem whatever it may be, but nothing happens. The situation gets worse or else it just stays stagnant. Why? Because some element isn't working with the rest. In most cases the thing that is out-of-sync is us, because we say things with our mouth that we really aren't saying with our heart. We need to ask ourselves, "What I really want in my heart, is it really right or is it self-serving?" This is where the higher self becomes involved. If we're being too self-serving, the higher self is going to block that prayer because what we're doing in essence is asking the higher power, God, to witness to a falsehood.

Those individuals who have reached that point where what they are saying with their mouth is the final declaration of what they have in their heart and in their higher self, have made a complete connection so that the power or those vibrations are flowing out and are connecting with others who are sending out that same vibration. And that combined energy then begins to work in the world. The dissolution of the Soviet Union and the reunification of Germany, the removal of the Berlin wall, are the result of prayer, the combined prayers of many. Man, if left to his own devices such as his intellect and his physical activities, will only facilitate the deterioration of the conditions of his world. With the implementation of proper prayer, the heart and the higher self are connected in a godly pursuit for a godly resolution to the problems. Now, we have a much more powerful force being applied to a situation than just man's mere intellect and physical activities. The perfect formula for a prayer situation is the alignment of the higher self, the heart, man's intelligence, and his efforts. This is the secret to powerful prayers.

Prayer can only be answered when it's a just prayer and when we are willing to work with the situation. How do we work with the situation? We have to be careful not to become a "gimme" person, with our prayers always becoming some form of "God gimme this, God gimme that." God doesn't give us anything if we aren't willing to do our part. We have to accept what He has laid out before us. The question then comes to mind, "Well, does that mean pain and suffering too?" There's no pain and suffering on our table that God has prepared for us. The pain and suffering come when we don't accept what's laid before us. In essence, pain and suffering come from the rejection of the gifts that God has given to us. Accept with gratitude what God offers you in answer to your prayers.

When we ask God's assistance in answering a prayer, we have to be willing to make the changes within our sphere of existence to help that prayer come about. If we don't, it isn't going to work. As an example, a husband and wife are having marital trouble. The husband prays, "I wish this would get straightened out so I can go on with my life." The wife is saying, "I pray that this gets straightened out so I can either go on with my life or else continue on with the marriage." They are both praying, but nothing really happens. The marriage is in a stagnant state where both of them are held down or what is worse, they dissolve the marriage. Why, if both are praying, why doesn't it work? It's because they aren't taking the necessary first step. They aren't working together to come to a solution. You can ask God for all kinds of things but if you don't work with the situation, nothing will happen. Let's continue on with our example. In working with the situation, you have to set yourself aside and say: "How have I acted in this? What have been my contributions to the problem?" Don't worry about the faults of the other person. You have to ask yourself. Then if you want a resolution either to mend the marriage or to sever the relationship completely, you have to determine which is the right thing to do and then you have to act accordingly, without vengeance, without malice, without blaming the other person. You have to assume the responsibility for your part and, to be on the safe side, accept a little bit more, just in case you're not totally honest with yourself. Then if you work within those parameters the prayer is going to be answered. It may not be answered exactly the way you want it to be but the problem will resolve itself so the situation is better than it was.

Now, does the resolution to the problem take place beyond our range of participation? Complete resolution comes to the degree that we are willing to participate in the accomplishment of the prayer. The more we bring the situation and our life into accord with the prayer the more complete the prayer will be answered.

The Council always advocates: When you pray, meditate. Prayer is asking; meditation is listening. Sometimes we can receive insight into what the real problem is or into what mode of action we should take if instead of saying: "God, give me this!" we remain silent and listen. Most people don't want to take that time because they know that if they listen, there may be something they are going to have to do, and nine times out of ten, it's the very thing they don't want to do. Then you have to ask yourself why. Maybe, whatever it is we aren't willing to do is the source of the problem.

When we pray for things to be resolved, we have to be very careful that the resolution we're praying for isn't self-serving because when we pray for something we can't pray over the right of another individual. For example, a person is sick, and has had a long life of terrible suffering, terrible pain, and we pray, "God please alleviate this pain and suffering of this person. This is a good person." We can't overpray that person's right. By that I mean we can't force a solution that person does not accept. If that suffering is a need within that person, we can't correct it. Possibly, if we are praying for the person's health to improve, that prayer may not be answered by an improvement in health but by an improvement in the problem that has caused the bad health. The underlying problem may be an emotional inability to accept reality. The sickness the individual is undergoing might be considered in their mind a legitimate way to avoid that reality. The prayer then might not affect the illness, but may help with the underlying problem, the inability to accept reality. Although we should not attempt to override an individual's rights, we still have the obligation to pray for a condition to improve or, at least, for that individual to become more fulfilled or happy.

There are some attitudes in the metaphysical field that say we should not pray for someone who is sick because that is their karma and we may be in-

terfering with their karmic debt. This is utter nonsense. If a person's karmic debt is the cause of an illness, praying for the illness to be corrected will not
be interfering with their karmic debt. To make this
clear let's examine the Divine Principle of cause and
effect. The illness is the effect of the karmic debt
which is the cause. By praying for the effect or the
illness to improve, that energy is directed by the individual who is sick to the cause or the karmic debt.
Thus, we are working at a level that we are not even
aware of. Or one may say, in this particular example,
we have the cart before the horse. We are dealing
with the effect and the individual then can utilize
that prayer vibration to deal with the cause.

Prayer is a very complicated situation and in a
way it's good that we don't realize how complicated
it is. If we did we would be so discouraged we
wouldn't pray. But the beauty of prayer is that in
our ignorance we can work greater miracles than we
can with knowledge, because we work from the
heart then and not the intellect.

Remember that the solution that you pray for
may not be the solution you receive. Be careful that
your ego doesn't demand that the problem be resolved as you think it should be. The resolution is
what you want, though it may not come in the manner you want it. The Divine Influence can assist us
when we ask for it in correcting situations far better
than what we think. It is a benefit not only for the
person we're praying for but also for ourself. We
can receive far greater benefits when the prayer is

resolved in ways other than the way we thought it should be resolved. We can eliminate the role of the ego by accepting the solution provided by the Divine.

Prayer is a marvelous thing. It's your first tool for working miracles, and if you are praying for the welfare of someone else, and you are doing it from the heart and with no self-serving interest you will be surprised how powerful a prayer can be.

If you can laugh
As you are now,
Believe us
That joy of the heart
Only magnifies
Once you leave the body behind,
And it is not unspiritual
To laugh,
Because as you grow in spirituality,
More joy fills your heart.

The truth has many doors
so that all believers who knock
will be welcomed in.

Chapter 20

The Divine Guarantees An Answer

Life today is like living inside a tornado. We get up in the morning and we are propelled into a whirlwind of activities, impossible schedules, outrageous costs, and what seems to us to be insurmountable problems. We are pulled from the right, we are pulled from the left; we are pulled from the top and we are pulled from the bottom. It is like being put onto a rack and stretched to our absolute limits. Not only has our schedule reached the point of a near killing pace, we must also be on guard as to our personal safety as we move through this maelstrom of activities. At the end of our workday we are physically exhausted and emotionally spent. Yet we must find the endurance to continue on with our personal life. We have been conditioned into a mindset of instant answers, actions, and desire fulfillment. In this bedlam of existence we must be able to find the time to develop a continuity, a tranquility, and a calm in which to bring some normalcy to our personal lives and family.

We try to bring calmness and security to our personal lives, but life is not as accommodating as we would hope. Many times we must face problems for which we need hope, strength, and a solution. Where do we seek out this support? Some individuals look to the stars hoping that astrology will give them the answer. Other individuals will seek out fortunetellers or psychics hoping for some reassurance, some support, some insight. There are individuals who will seek guidance from the spiritual realms in the form of departed friends, family, guides, or masters. And then there are those who will turn to a Tarot deck or use the runes as another source for some guidance for problems that they may have in their life. The reliability of these avenues is questionable. Even with those that are authentic, we can never be sure that the guidance is wise or from a dependable source.

Where can we gain the answer to the problems in our life, and be 100% sure that it is of the highest nature? That is, how can we be certain that it is the very best guidance or advice that we can gain? Some years ago during one of the Trances we received a very simple suggestion on how to insure guidance and be assured that it is of the highest quality. Such guidance is at your fingertips any time you choose. It doesn't take extensive preparation. It doesn't cost you anything. And the answer to your problem can be almost instantaneous. There are times that you may have to stop and think for a period of time, but the answer is there for you. It is a matter of understanding. There is only one item that you must have. For the Christian it would be the Bible. For those of other religions, it would be a book of what is generally recognized as their holy writings. So whatever religion you accept, you have a source of guidance, you have a book. Let's examine this process from the Western or Christian concept, but this process is applicable to all religions.

Whatever your problem is, sit down in a quiet place and concentrate on it. Simply say to yourself, my problem is this. Think about it. Ask for guidance. Ask for a solution to the problem that will bring happiness, benefit, and productivity to all concerned. Now it is very important to take a few minutes to concentrate on the problem. Then take the Bible, hold it between both hands on its binding edge, and, after concentrating, allow the Bible to fall open wherever it will. Place your hand someplace on one of the pages. Do this with your eyes closed so you eliminate any possible subconscious influence. Once the Bible has opened up, let your hand move of its own accord to either the right or left-hand page. In other words, do not attempt to direct the hand to one page or the other. You may want to simply allow your hand to drop to the page. Make sure that the index finger is extended so that you will be pointing to a particular verse. It is important to make sure that you do not deliberately place your finger at a particular position on the page. Simply let the natural falling of the hand determine the placement of the index finger. Wherever the index finger lands, read that verse and within that context, you will have the answer to your problem. This is an absolute guarantee. It has never failed for me and it has never failed for others who have used it.

In many cases the verse itself will give you a very direct solution to the problem. In those situations where the understanding of that particular verse and how it applies to you and your situation is not so clear, it may be necessary to read a number of verses before and after the verse you are pointing to. This will give you a better understanding of that particular verse. In some cases you may have to read the entire chapter, but most chapters in the Bible are very short, and this would only take a few minutes. The reason it may be necessary to read more than just the verse that your finger is touching, is that it will give you a better understanding of the meaning of that verse and the context in which it is written, because this will also give you more understanding into the solution of your problem. Remember, the more knowledge and understanding one has, the more tools one has to work with. If you are willing to apply what the verse indicates, this will take care of the problem. This means you must apply it in your life, not just in your thoughts.

Why does this work? The first thing we have to understand is that everything in life or creation, whether it is the material aspects or spiritual aspects, is connected. Nothing is isolated. In this fact of reality, that all things are connected, there are bridges or pathways or avenues that we can travel that can bring us to these different points or opportunities. Some of these avenues are simple little actions or thoughts, attitudes, or frames of mind, sometimes referred to as altered states of consciousness. Using a holy book or a book of scripture is one such pathway. If you recognize a collection of writings that epitomize a godly spiritual nature, then somewhere in that recognition you also recognize the authority or the source (not necessarily the writer.) By placing your confidence in that source, you then open up a bridge to the influence of that source. Therefore, if you recognize the Bible as the instructions of your God, then you are opening a connection between you and that Divine Source. Whatever you recognize as God, if it be the true God, there will always be guidance of the highest quality and nature available to you.

Let us analyze the procedure of this particular avenue of connecting with the Divine Source and the solutions offered there. First, we take a few moments to concentrate on the problem, we focus in on it. We ask a solution to that problem that will benefit all concerned. We do not ask that it be solved in a way that will suit us, but we ask for a solution that will be of benefit to all concerned. In so doing we put no barriers, no hindrances or stipulations to the guidance that comes to us.

The next step is allowing the Bible to naturally fall open to where it will, and randomly allowing our hand to drop to a particular place on one of the pages. How does this activity or this action work? If you recognize the Divine as the ultimate Source, the ultimate Power, then you also have to accept the fact that there is nothing impossible to this Source, to God. Would anybody really think that it is a tremendous task for this Divine Power to open a book to a particular page and allow a hand to drop to a particular portion of that page? Some may ask: Wouldn't it be possible to willfully put your hand at the top or the bottom or the middle of the page? Yes, anything is possible. But remember to allow the hand to fall naturally. If you have deliberately influenced this portion of this activity, upon reading the verse it will become obvious that you have deliberately influenced the movement of your hand. And if you have read that verse in context, it will be very obvious that you have influenced that process. It is important to do this with your eyes closed so there won't be an interference.

Some people may ask, is there only one verse in the Bible that will give me the answer to my problem? The answer here is no. There are many, many verses in the Bible that hold the solution, that hold the answers, to all the problems of mankind, regardless of how big or how small they may be. Even if there might be only one verse that held the solution to your problem, it would be of no great effort for God to choose that one verse. In actuality, although there may be many verses that would offer the proper solution to your problem, the Divine Presence, knowing you as well as He does, will choose the verse that is the best for you and where you are at at that point in time.

Here are some suggestions that will make for a better physical condition under which this process is used. First, make sure that you are in a fairly peaceful or quiet situation, with a limited amount of external distraction. The next condition is to use a new Bible, if at all possible. You do not want to use one that has bits of paper or cards tucked in amongst the many pages. If we use an older Bible, many times the Bible will naturally fall open to the same pages because the binding has been cracked or worn. I suggest that if you purchase a Bible for this practice, use it only for this practice. Also, if you are using a new Bible, fan the pages a number of times, that is, flip through the entire Bible using your thumb across the edge so that the pages open freely and are not stuck to one another. Do this from front to back a half dozen times and from back to front another half dozen times.

The next step in preparing your Bible is to divide the Bible into approximately eight sections. This is approximate—you don't need to count the pages. Deliberately open that Bible widely at each of the eight divisions. This will help to loosen the binding edge without causing it to crack. You may, if you choose, gently press the length of the page where they come together at the binding edge. This is the only preparation necessary for this connection between you and your God.

One more suggestion to the process is this. Before you concentrate on your problem, take a few minutes to write out your problem on paper. Write it as simply as possible. This will help to formulate it in your thoughts or in your prayer or in your meditation prior to the rest of the process. This is not absolutely necessary, but it will help you in a clearer understanding of the problem.

All creation is connected, and in this process of connection there are certain avenues, bridges, pathways, that unite all of creation. These are for us to use. They are not necessary for the Divine, but they are necessary for us because as we discover these bridges, these pathways, we must first have had to achieve a specific understanding, a specific insight, a specific awareness, and the faith to trust in such a child-like action and belief. Remember, it is the child that the Divine encompasses in His Arms and will hold to His Bosom.

If you do not judge others
You cannot be judged.
If you love others,
Then the only thing
That can be returned to you
Is love.

The one who loves you cannot bring you happiness with his love, if he first does not find happiness in loving.

Chapter 21

Compassion Where None Exists

Experiences in life can be very cruel and unfair, but man can bring a kindness and a fairness to this experience we call life.

A while ago I was asked by a psychiatrist to speak to a small group of patients who were terminally ill. He had asked me to talk to them about the need to have hope, the need to tap into that inner strength, and the desire to draw on the spiritual aspects of our nature that give us the will to live.

On that particular evening for the better part of an hour I made the effort to establish the motivation in these people that would lead to a more comfortable life and the ability to deal with their conditions.

Afterwards, I had the privilege of talking with these people individually, having the time to discuss their personal situations with them. At the end of that evening, I had no idea what would transpire only a short time in the future.

Some months later I was going to the hospital to visit a family member. Having the room number firmly set in my mind, I confidently walked into a room only to be surprised with the fact that the face that I saw was not the face I expected. However, the face I looked at seemed strangely familiar. I was a bit startled. Even though the face looked familiar I couldn't place it. From the tone of his greeting, it was quite obvious that he knew who I was. I found myself in a very awkward position. I was expecting to see family and instead I was facing someone I really couldn't place. Fumbling for words through this awkward situation, I finally realized that this was one of the people that I had talked to at the request of the psychiatrist. I was immediately interested in how he was and what the circumstances were that brought him to the hospital. It was quite evident to me that this kind man was very depressed. Knowing the devastation of depression, I decided to spend some additional time with him, listening to what he had to say and attempting to encourage him and give him hope. (For those of you who have never experienced deep depression, it is like being cast into a deep, dark hole or placed in a cage that you cannot escape from. You can only hope for some light in that hole or the sound of a key in the lock of the cage.)

After a period of about two hours he seemed to be in a better frame of mind. I told him that I would have to leave if I were going to visit my relative. I left on a light-hearted note saying it was quite a co-incidence to walk into the wrong room only to meet someone I had met before. The man asked me if I would please come back and visit him again, and I said that I would try to get back soon. He attempted to pin me down to a more specific time such as "This week?" I told him that I could not give him a specific time but I would try very hard to get back to see how he was doing.

As I was leaving the hospital, I happened to run into the psychiatrist. I mentioned to him that I had accidentally walked into the room of this man. We chuckled at the word "accidentally," both believing that there is no such thing as an accident. Knowing the situation and the doctor that he is, I wasn't surprised when he seized the opportunity to ask me if I would make it a point to visit his patient again. I said yes and he requested that I give him a call before I visited the gentleman. He wanted me to deliver a letter to the patient. I assured him that I would. Since it was near the end of the week, I decided that I would visit his patient the first part of the following week. When I called the psychiatrist, he informed me that there would be an envelope that contained a letter at the information desk and that I should pick it up. The only information I had concerning this letter was that it was from the aunt of the patient. The circumstances of why it should be sent to the doctor and not to the patient were never given to me.

I delivered the letter to the patient and during the course of my conversation with him, I learned of his situation, which the doctor later verified.

This very kind and innocent human being was dying of AIDS and was dying of this disease all alone. He contracted this disease from his wife. Although he was faithful, the same could not be said of the wife. Her promiscuous lifestyle while he was at work was the avenue through which she contracted the disease, and in turn she infected her husband. In a short period of time, his health began to fail. Upon seeing his physician, he was diagnosed with an active case of AIDS. During a consultation between the wife, the husband, and the doctor, the wife admitted to her infidelities. She tested HIV positive but still was in good health. As the husband's condition deteriorated quickly, she decided to leave him. She left him on his own to survive the best he could.

I also learned from the patient that he had a brother and sister. Once they found out his condition they chose to have as little contact with him as possible. The only thing that he got from his mother and father was the chastisement that they had warned him against marrying this woman. They chose to ignore his emotional and physical suffering. His brother and sister would visit about once a month. His parents once and sometimes twice a week. As I looked at the card holder on the wall in his room, at the top were two cards signed, "From your parents." At the bottom were at least a dozen cards and letters many pages long signed, "With love and prayers, Your Aunt."

I also discovered that the psychiatrist had talked to the patient's parents, brother, and sister, attempting to encourage them to offer their emotional and spiritual support. With this help, the patient would have a much better chance to stave off some of the vicious attacks of his disease. But because of the lack of love, compassion, and understanding, this man received nothing but silence and distance from those who supposedly loved him, who did in fact love him before he innocently became a victim. The brother and sister feared being even in the same room with their brother. The parents rationalized their coldness by the fact that they had warned him against the marriage. Consequently, the man had practically no visitors at all. His room was empty of any flowers, any plants. All he had were the two cards from his mother and father and the many cards and letters from his aunt.

I visited this man a number of times. On the last occasion I went into the room with another letter from his aunt. I noticed he looked extremely weak and very tired, but he managed a small smile. I asked him how he felt. He said he didn't think he could make it any longer. I said I would read his aunt's letter to him. I had hoped that her words would be uplifting to him. After finishing the letter I told him that he had to fight a little harder.

He said, "I've fought long enough just to see my only friend one more time."

He looked at me, there was a smile on his face, he sighed very deeply, and life left.

I hit the call button and asked for someone to be sent in immediately. The nurse came in, saw me holding his hand and the first words she said were, "Don't touch him. Don't you know that he has AIDS?" I said to her, "Try and do something for him."

She put on her rubber gloves, checked his pulse, placed her stethoscope on his chest, and said, "He's dead. You'd better leave now."

Why did this man have to die without his family around him? Why was it this man only had letters from his aunt that rang with any kind of warmth? Why did this man have to look at practically a stranger and call him friend?

Whoever said life was to be fair? Life is a test of the quality of man. Because of man's lack of respect for himself and his fellow man, life has become an exercise in man's inhumanity to man. Life is now a test of how brave and courageous we are. It is a test of our compassion and our love. Only through this compassion, this love, can we bring a fairness to life. Only through this compassion and love can we dissolve away man's inhumanity to man. This can only be accomplished on a one-to-one basis. Only when we are able to climb out of our own self-indulgence will we be able to see the need that others have. And it is only through our compassion and love that we will be able to answer the needs of others. Where is your love and compassion? Where is your effort in dissolving the darkness that exists in this experience we call life?

Let us celebrate the rediscovery of compassion and love that each of us are capable of. Let us most importantly learn to give freely of this compassion and love to whomever may need it. To those in need, hope is the essence that gives us courage to face the next minute, the next hour, the next day.

May the Blessings of our Lord and God
Be acceptable to your souls.
May the Joy of our experience,
And our relationship with the Divine Source,
Be part of your experiences,
And your state of existence.
May the hosts of Heaven
Always be permitted to share
Their Joy and their Strength
With each and every one of you.

All parts of life are connected
to the powerful creative forces
of the Divine Presence.

Chapter 22

Time and Destiny

Even though we appear to be living second by second and minute by minute, we have, in fact, already left the material existence and are living in our reward. This is because in actuality we are all living in the now, but for our comprehension events must appear to occur in a linear progression. The linear aspect of time is necessary for our conscious mind. It allows souls the opportunity to mesh their life patterns, to work in parallel for a brief period, and to get into position for each event in our lives.

Time is not as smooth-flowing and consistent as we perceive it to be. However, for the proper experiencing of physical creation it is necessary that we view the passage of events in a one, two, three succession. Such a succession is, in fact, when viewed from the soul's perspective of the ever-present now, understood as a total unit of six. The soul views a series of moments as one complete picture. We do the same to a degree when reviewing past experiences in our mind. Many of the details are missing or incomplete but the experience will be viewed by the mind's eye as one complete thought or event.

The Council has said, "There is a progression at all times, but with the Divine the unity of that progression is observed along with the actions of that progression, where in your ability to observe, to experience, you do not see the unity of it, consequently, you see everything as separate isolated episodes, consequently, you see time or are aware of it."

The All-Knowing mind of God is totally independent of time. St. Augustine, placing time in its proper relationship to the activity of God, writes, "His eternity is not an everlastingness but, rather, an existence that is altogether independent of time. God therefore sees the whole of history in a manner similar to that in which we view the present, and from this point of view one is not easily tempted to suppose that God's knowledge imposes any determination on things to come."

God's perspective on time versus ours can be demonstrated in this manner: From the top of a snow-covered hill we have a panoramic view of the surrounding area. We can't see everything but we can get a good look around. God, on the other hand, when viewing the world, is capable of climbing the very highest mountain that exists. From there His view is infinitely better than ours. Similarly, God views all of history as a single, complete thought. Man's view by comparison is very, very limited. It is so limited that he cannot fully grasp the concept of time and the ever-present now. He also finds it hard to imagine how the soul utilizes the variableness of time to bring him spiritual growth.

In defining time The Council has said, "Time is only this: it gives you a reference point in reality, in awareness, where you and another may meet at a predetermined time for a predetermined experience. In other words, it is nothing more than a signpost on a corner of nothing where you have agreed to meet . . ."

Time is an activity of the mind, an agreed upon reference point where souls meet and cooperate for each event in the physical existence. It could be a conscious meeting such as, "I'll be meeting you at 5:30" or "The game starts at seven." It could also be an event scheduled by two people at a soul level. At the soul level the scenario could go something like this: Your consciousness wishes to revive an old relationship. The one soul communicates its desire to meet the other. "How about meeting me at the local drugstore?" the first soul says. The second replies, "That's not good for me. I don't get along with the druggist." The first says, "Well, how about the grocery store. I'll be in the produce section looking at carrots and you can be there to pick up some lettuce." "Fine, that's fine," says the second. "I didn't have anything planned for the day." So the two souls have arranged a "chance" meeting at the grocery store on Saturday morning. While renewing their acquaintance they discover a similar interest in something that brings their friendship back to life, thereby bringing them closer together. An agreed upon time and place was necessary. Any time would do just as long as both agreed. Of course, at a soul level, beings would not really find it necessary to communicate verbally. It would be an instantaneous knowing by the higher consciousness. One of the souls would make its desire known and the other would agree to fulfill the request immediately.

We could surmise that the "chance" meeting at the grocery store was not planned but was an opportunity that became probable. From our perspective that may appear to be the case. However, we could just as easily say that the event was planned long before these two souls ever entered physical creation. This assumption would be just as correct. There was always a probability that they would reestablish their relationship. It was a predetermined option. The souls could follow their original plan to reestablish their friendship or deviate from it up to the moment of its actual occurrence. The deviation from the meeting does not in any way preclude the possibility that it might not occur at some future time under a different set of circumstances, if the two agree that something will be gained.

We have a degree of comprehension of God's perspective on time and how He knows our past, present and future because in His view all of physical existence is one complete event. Also, we understand that His knowledge of future events does not infringe on our opportunity to make totally free-willed choices as we go through life. It is important that we remember that the needs and desires of others become a tempering factor in our ability to exercise our freedom of choice. To varying degrees our choices are modified by our willingness to cooperate with others and help facilitate their needs. We definitely predetermine some of our earthly experiences, but those plans are often altered to some degree as we move closer to the actual experiencing of the event. Since we have the freedom to make choices within an environment of cooperation with others, we return again to the question: "How can events be known before they occur and yet not be predestined?" All souls have the free will to change their plans. Yet, as an event moves closer to fruition the final determination of the event is less likely to be altered from what had been agreed upon. As future events develop they become more clearly defined as time moves closer to the actual occurrence of the event.

An example. Suppose we are back on the top of the snow-covered hill. This time we make a snowball and start rolling the snowball down the hill. Initially the snowball is very small, and therefore has very little force of its own. The direction of travel is easily changed as our will determines. As the snowball goes down the hill it gathers more snow and grows larger, therefore it gains momentum. Now it is becoming far more difficult to change the snowball's course. Eventually, if it becomes large enough, the snowball will be impossible to control. Most importantly, as the snowball gains momentum it becomes much easier to predict the snowball's final destination.

Similarly, an event about to occur is much easier to predict than one many years in the future. The impending event has gained momentum and there is less chance of its path being influenced by variables. Its destiny is eventually set. An impending war situation is an example of an event gaining momentum. We realize that wars do not randomly occur. History has taught us that they grow from small incidents. Hatred builds and people do things and say things that cause tension. Momentum increases. After a point it may become impossible for any one person or group of persons to prevent the war. It becomes inevitable that one side must overpower the other. Whether it be a snowball rolling down a hill or the hatred of a few people, once out of control, its course may not be altered. Thus, one could say that the future is predictable or predetermined, but only predetermined in the sense that the influencing conditions have now created what is the most probable, natural and obvious conclusion.

To ensure our destiny we must look closely at the conditions that we are setting up in our lives now. Those conditions create probabilities that could eventually develop our destinies. If happiness is a desirable factor in our future then the seeds for that happiness must be planted now. This will give the time to nurture those seeds into all the happiness we desire.

This Infinite Father constantly
Has His Arms outstretched
Begging you to return to His Bosom.
He understands your humanness.
He wants you to understand
Your godliness.
He wants you to realize
That you are a great, loving entity
That can create all the benefits
That the world needs
For a godly peace in creation.

To feel on the inside
what you show on the outside
is to be in harmony with yourself.

Chapter 23

Sexual Incarnations

At a purely soul level, we do not look at life in terms of male and female roles, but we look at the masculine and feminine genders in a more profound way, and that is as avenues of creation and growth for our at-one-ment with the Divine Source. We, in our truest state as conscious state beings, do not consider either the male or female gender to be significantly more important than the other. We view these genders as being equal. They offer us different varieties of choices for our growth. At the deepest levels of our awareness, we are fully aware that the male and female genders are nothing more than garments that we place on our being so we may experience life from two different perspectives.

Although reincarnation is not a principal thought of Christianity, it is a major spiritual concept of two thirds of the world, and for this reason it is necessary that we address it. At each incarnation we experience, when we return to the earth plane to experience life again, we return with a specific purpose, and that is to correct the karmic debt or karmic situation that we have incurred for ourselves. Do we choose to do that as one gender over the other? Not necessarily. We will move into whatever available avenue is most expedient for us. Each life we experience can be looked at as a means to an end. Each life is a way in which we can further our at-one-ment with our Divine Source. If choosing a lifetime as a male will accomplish this for us, then, of course, this will be our first choice. If a lifetime as a female will serve us better, then that will be our first choice. There may be some exceptions dealing with certain karmic debts that we may have incurred where it may be necessary to choose a particular gender to correct that karmic debt in an expedient manner. But this, of course, is the exception. We must remember that the soul itself is androgynous, neither male nor female, but a blending of the two.

There are types of karmic debts that we incur as a male and there are types of karmic debts that we incur as a female. Which of these types of karmic debts we deal with in a particular lifetime depends on whether we choose to incarnate as a male or as a female. At a soul level, when we decide to work on a particular karmic debt, that becomes one of the factors determining what our gender will be. This is not necessarily a hard and fast rule for reincarnating. However, there are not certain or separate karmic debts for the male and separate karmic debts for the female. In actuality, they overlap each other. This gives us another avenue of choice. Suppose for some reason we chose to work out a karmic debt we created as a male, and there is not a specific or sufficient situation to incarnate as a male. We can correct that karmic debt through the female gender.

An example. Suppose there was a father who was cold and distant toward his son. He was also very stern in his relationship with his son. This in turn created a hostile environment between the father and son. In a following lifetime, the soul that manifested as the father could then manifest as a female who would undergo the experience of childbirth, bonding very closely with that child. The soul who originally incarnated as the father would be able to correct the karmic situation between him and his son by using the female gender in order to reestablish a bond with the child.

This choice may not be as efficient for us as the male body would have been. Nevertheless, the opportunity to make the correction is still there. The opportunity to incarnate as a female and correct the karmic debt may not be as efficient, but it is more expedient than waiting for a suitable situation to incarnate as a male. It still is a means to the end.

Can we choose one gender over the other more frequently, and possibly get ourselves out of balance or not deal with our karmic debts in an appropriate or efficient manner? There are some natural governing elements to protect us from this situation; there is a limit to the number of times we can reincarnate consecutively as a male or a female. We can correct our karmic debts as either gender, but in the overall plan of growth or spiritual at-one-ment, there are governing conditions that will prevent us from emphasizing one aspect of our androgynous nature over the other. We must remember that as androgynous beings we must keep the masculine nature and the feminine nature in balance. To do so, this means we cannot reach perfection through repeated incarnations of one gender over the other. We will not be able to solely concentrate on the masculine nature or feminine nature in order to reach at-one-ment with the Divine Source. To reach at-one-ment necessitates equal opportunity for both of our natures.

So is it best, in order to keep the androgynous entity in balance, to incarnate as a male in one lifetime and as a female in the next, and to go through this alternating pattern in order to reach perfection? We have a latitude in making choices. If we choose, we may come back a number of times as a male or a number of times as a female. We also have the choice of going back and forth from male to female. To keep a balance of the masculine and feminine natures within us does not dictate the necessity of alternating lifetimes.

We should not place any significance on what gender we are utilizing in a particular lifetime. We cannot assume that if we are a male that the female aspect of our androgynous being is in perfect balance. The more accurate assumption would be that it most likely was an appropriate opening or lifetime that we could utilize. We cannot safely assume anything beyond this point, that it was an expedient lifetime for us.

One might be tempted to assume that there is an imbalance in the soul that reincarnates as a male but has an effeminate nature, or that reincarnates as a female but acts masculine. But just because a man may be effeminate or a woman may be masculine does not indicate that there is a spiritual problem. Such observations may be based solely on what we as a society deem normal. Just because we believe a certain standard of behavior is normal does not make it so. Our decisions as to what is normal and what is not normal are not necessarily based in spirituality. More than likely they will be based on society's attitudes or decisions on what may be considered proper or normal. We are not in a position to judge nor do we have the right to form judgmental attitudes toward others.

The condition of an effeminate male does not necessarily mean the soul is out of balance. Two possible explanations come to mind. The first is that this individual soul simply does not fit the mold in which society wishes to cast him. Therefore, society views this individual as an anomaly, when in fact this individual is not an anomaly. This individual simply does not fit into a traditional mold of society's making. The second possibility is that the individual chose such a condition to experience the wrath of society. Such an individual comes into life in order to give others the opportunity to make a choice. The first choice would be to ridicule, to humiliate, to ostracize, and to condemn. These are all actions of a judgmental society. The second choice we would have as individuals and as a society, would be to show consideration. This would indicate respect, acceptance, compassion, and unconditional love. What right do we have to pass judgment on any individual? The only rights we have concerning other individuals are to show compassion and to show love without reservation.

One might wonder if spiritual growth can be attained simply by balancing the two sides of our androgynous nature. No, the important factor is not whether we balance the male and female aspects. What is important, whether male or female, is the kind of life that we live. Is that life one of productivity? Is it a loving life, a life that is filled with love? If these two activities are a part of our life, then it is necessary for us to be able to draw on both aspects of our nature. In order to love unconditionally, we must demonstrate a strength of conviction, which is the male aspect, and a sensitivity and compassion, which is the female aspect.

What we do in this particular lifetime that we are now living is more important than whether we are utilizing a male body or a female body. In actuality, we can learn our lessons, correct our karmic debts, regardless of whether we are male or female. The different genders simply offer us different avenues through which we can share our abilities to love unconditionally.

You see,
What you must begin to understand
In the life that Christ
Has showed you you must live
Is that His Life was not,
How shall we put it,
A life of talking;
His was a life of action.
He had a living concern
For those around Him,
And He demonstrated that concern.
Certainly He prayed,
But He allowed that prayer
To live in the world
By demonstrating His love
And His concern
For those around Him;
Having the time
For those who had need.

Do all things with great love,
even the small things,
for the small things show
how great the love truly is.

Chapter 24

Little Secrets to Spiritual Growth

For most of us, the most appropriate epitaph would be, "Too little, too late."

This epitaph does not belong to us because of the winds of fate but more probably because of our own self-indulgent blindness. Strong words of indictment, but bear with me, for I am talking more of myself than anyone else.

Some years ago I had a near death experience. Upon realizing that I was dead, and having gone through the traditional tunnel and meeting of relatives and spiritual figures, I reached the point where I had to review my life. I was very apprehensive when the review came to certain aspects of my life, particularly my early years, fearful of what my sins would cost me. I recall at that split second, if I can use such terms in an experience that does not actually relate to time, I recalled a few occasions wherein I felt I would definitely have to pay a price. As my life began to unfold before my eyes, and I moved through those experiences feeling and experiencing each second of my life, not just at a mental level but at an emotional and physical level, I was quite surprised as I passed through those events I thought would surely cost me, to find that they passed by with relative ease compared with what was to come. It was much like a moment of profound sadness.

The very things that I considered so lightly or barely considered at all, I was soon to realize would be the very things that would wrench my heart from my chest and cause me the greatest pain. A deeply mournful sadness overwhelmed me to the point where I could barely endure myself for the shame I felt.

What were these experiences that brought me to my knees? What were these things that were so hideous and painful? What were they? They were the little things: I passed by a little old woman with a cane and forgot to hold the door open for her. I was too busy with my own thoughts. I forgot to phone a friend to ask what the doctor had to say about his last visit. I forgot to say thank you to a gentleman who held the door open for me. I forgot to kiss my mother one day when I was leaving her home because I was in a hurry. I forgot to hug my dad because I was thoughtless. I forgot to say, "I love you" to someone I should have said those words to. I didn't think of paying a compliment to someone who deserved it and needed it. I forgot to be courteous. I forgot to be mannerly. I forgot to think, to think about what the other person might need.

These are all little acts, and some of you may think they are trivial, non-important, non-essential. You may say, "What do they really have to do with spirituality?" Let me say this: The list you have just read has everything to do with spirituality because it IS spirituality. One thing I learned from my near death experience that I will share with you is this: The big jobs in life that are our responsibility to take care of, after all is said and done, are the easiest steps in spirituality. But the true spiritual essence of an individual truly shines forth in the little acts that we rarely think of or that we too often take for granted. The little efforts of kindness, politeness, and respect. These are the acts that show whether we are truly spiritual at the depth of our soul or whether we are simply spiritual on a superficial level. Remembering the little things demonstrates a state of consciousness. It reveals the compassion, the love, the empathy, the caring, and the respect that we have for others.

Be very cognizant of your actions and very cautious in large·wrong-doings, for you will definitely experience a tremendous amount of remorse and shame. You will feel the pain and sadness that your actions have caused others. But be even more aware of the little acts that demonstrate compassion and respect for others, for these are the events that will cause the greatest sadness. Your self-worth will ultimately be equal to the small acts of consideration and kindness that you demonstrate in your day-to-day lives. It is those seemingly insignificant little happenings that we experience a dozen times a day that offer us the greatest spiritual growth and the greatest spiritual bounties. The little acts will allow us to walk into eternity draped in garlands of bounty and armfuls of precious spiritual gifts.

I was blessed with a second chance. I could return with this understanding and the opportunity to change. My hopes and prayers are that you in some way will come to the same realization that I was granted, and venture forth into a new consciousness of love, so that we may all walk together arm in arm into eternity draped in the spiritual garlands that we justly deserve and which are rightfully ours.

Look on some evening
When the sky is clear
And the stars are bright.
Look up into the heavens
And see as far as the eye can see.
If you can feel the magnitude
Of what you are seeing,
If you can feel the immensity
of what you are seeing,
If you can see and feel the beauty
And the glory of what you are seeing,
Then you have some idea
Of what you will be creating,
And yet at the same time the creation
That you will be working on
Will be you, yourself.

Epilogue*

Here I am lost in this dream that man calls life.
The life inside of me ebbs and flows with a desire
For something more than this long winter's day;
This long winter's day that is nothing more
Than a collage of drab lifeless grays.
One gray more lifeless than the other,
Punctuated by slashes of black that are totally void
    of life.
As I look to the sky, the churning gray clouds
Give no hint of a sun, only a dead moon.
It sheds no light, it is simply a gray ball;
There; in front of the churning roll of the
    darkening clouds.
The clouds relinquish their snow.
It does not fall, it drops directly to the ground
And covers the landscape with granules of varying
    shades of gray.

---

*In its most traditional sense an epilogue is a poem spoken by one of the actors to the audience at the end of a play. That sense is preserved here somewhat in this free-verse composition offered to the reader, not as a summary, but as an inspiration to further spiritual exploration. (Editor's note)

The winds, when they rise up,
Do not blow to and fro, they shove this way and
    that way.
This is man's life.
A life of deceptions, possessions and conquests.
It is not life but a lingering death.
My life, my reality, is not man's life or man's
    reality.
I look around, nothing moves
Save the snow that dropped to the ground.

All the things that I can see exist, and yet have no
    life.
At my feet is a small pool; it is filled with a watery
    slush.
Even this pool must be void of any life.
Wait, did my eyes see a movement
In that dark slurry of water and ice?
Again there is a motion, I put my hand in,
To search for what life might be there.
Something brushes my fingertip.
I move my hand around. Nothing. I withdraw it.
A motion, my hand in the water;
Something moves through my cupped hand and
    then is gone.
I keep still; It moves into my hand and pauses.
I gently close my hand around the life
And raise it from the water.
I look at the small form.
It is a small fish, almost lifeless.
I breathe my warm breath on it;

The fish moves as if to look at me.
Once again I touch it with my breath; it moves.
Its eyes are full of sadness and loneliness.
My heart is taken by such sadness and loneliness.
Holding the little fish, I look at this landscape of
    desolation,
This land of the living dead.
I look at the little fish; it has life in it.
I am alive, I am living.
This is not my reality, this is not our reality.
Home.

Home to our reality.
My consciousness takes flight and we travel
Through time and space towards the domain of
    true reality.
Cupped gently in my hand,
We leave the grays and blacks that man calls life.
We pass through the world of azure blue,
Then on to the royal blue.
Above to the midnight blue that is sprinkled
With countless lights that sparkle like diamonds.
On and on we travel through this domain.
I look at the little fish,
And I can see it does not have much time to live.
My heart aches; I do not want to lose my little
    one.
I will not let this happen.
I raise my voice to the Heavens above
And call forth the mightiest angels of Love
To assist me in my flight.

Comets of brilliant light
Propelled by great wings of gold appear.
They surround us, the little fish and me,
And buoy us up on their brilliance,
Carrying us at an immeasurable speed
Into the Great Light of lights.
We are set down at the edge of a small crystal
        clear pool.
My heart aches even more
As I look at the fish's ever weakening condition.
I want to give it part of my life, part of my soul.
I want the fish to live.
I breathe on the little fish,
Trying to give the breath of my life.
The little fish tries to respond; it is weak but it
        tries.
I place the little fish into the crystal clear water.
I call again for help from the angels of Love.

The angels appear
And let their brilliance touch the little fish.
It gives a small quiver
And then before my eyes a miracle begins to
        occur.
The little fish's tail starts to turn to a golden color;
It becomes a fish with a golden tail.
To my greater amazement, the golden color
        continues to cover the entire fish's body
Until it is now a beautiful golden fish.
Then one of the angels of Love proclaims,

"Only love can create. Take the golden fish from
    the water
And place it on the grass in front of you."
I do as I am told.
The angel continues,
"Place your finger to your lips and touch it to the
    fish.
Behold a creation through love."
Before my very eyes the golden fish rises up on its
    tail;
It begins to change into the form of a Being.
The form is perfect in every detail.
The golden locks that frame the face
And drape over the shoulders give the face an
    angelic beauty.
One element is missing; it appears to have no life.
The angel of Love once again proclaims,
"Only love can create.
Place your right hand to your heart
And then touch it to the heart of the one before
    you."
Again I do as I am told.
The moment I do this the figure begins to breathe,
The eyes open and the lips part in a smile.
The angel of Love pronounces,
"Only love can create.
Behold the transformation of a loving touch
From the heart of one, to the heart of the other,
Brings life and bonds the two souls.
Hear this, we announce to all creation
That these two are mates of the soul.

The doors to the gardens of Heaven open wide to
    them,
So that they may enter side by side,
That others may see what love is.
And as these two walk past the flowers of the
    Heavenly gardens,
Let those flowers bow as a sign of
    acknowledgment
To what love can create.
Let this be for all Eternity."
And so, side by side, the two enter the gardens of
    Heaven.
The true reality.
Their reality.
Home.

Life is a series of experiences. The only experiences that make life worthy and successful are those experiences that deal with giving and loving and then having that love returned to us. A caring love is the only act that can create a joyful life.

Loving can only begin when we first reach out to another, whether it be with a word or a touch. The act of love can be elevated to the ultimate experience when the love is extended from the heart of one individual, then accepted and returned by the heart of another. A soul may seek to find himself and never accomplish it. A soul may seek to find his God and never accomplish that. A soul may seek a friend and discover that not only has he found a friend but also has found himself and his God.

Love opens the gates to heaven where we are truly acknowledged for the quality that we have become, and the flowers of heaven bow in recognition of our accomplishment, love.

WILLIAM ALLEN LEPAR

index

T

U

V

W

Z

Table of First Lines
from The Council Quotes